A Boaters Gui(

by

Chris N. Deuchar

Based on a series of articles
first published in the newsletter of
the historic
Narrow Boat Owners Club

The historic
NARROW BOAT
OWNERS CLUB

Published by Chris N. Deuchar on behalf of the historic Narrow Boat Owners Club

© Chris N. Deuchar - except where otherwise credited

First published 1997
Revised Edition 2000 (minor corrections only)

Membership details of the Historic Narrow Boat Owners Club, and additional copies of this book, may be obtained from the author, c/o Nottingham University, Sutton Bonington Campus, Loughborough LE12 5RD.

Contact the author by email at:
Chris@Deuchars.co.uk

ISBN 0 9531512 0 4

Printed by Foxprint, Leicestershire, England

Acknowledgements

I am indebted in particular to the following for their assistance (and therefore encouragement!) in the preparation of this publication:-

The historic Narrow Boat Owners Club, J Bowles, D Daines, C W Groves, N Hill, N Hughes, R Wickson and to the innumerable others, whose names I have forgotten or never even knew, from whom I have acquired ideas and techniques over the years.

Special Thanks

To Harry Arnold (Waterway Images) for the cover photograph and those on pages 16, 18, 55 and 59, and Syd Arkless for that on page 13.

(All text, other photographs, drawings and graphic design by the author.)

1

CONTENTS

PREFACE

This book is not intended for the novice but for those with some boating experience who wish to refine their technique and learn some of the ways of the working boats, alongside new ways appropriate to today's leisure dominated waterways.

These ideas and comments resulted from casual observation around the country which led me to speculate that some boaters (including sometimes other NBOC members and myself) did not always have quite the control they should have over their craft. On a waterway system that is becoming increasingly populated by those whose distance in time and attitude gets further and further away from their working boat predecessors, I felt that there was a lot of valuable knowledge remaining unwritten, and which was disappearing, as well as being spread forever more thinly.

My own experience started with model boats. The first of these was built by my father as an unexpected Christmas present. This led to much model boat building of my own and play on the then commercially busy River Trent.

Having moved house and on reaching our 'teens, two neighbouring friends and I each built our own canoes. These PBK (Percy Blandford Kayak) canvas on wood designs, enabled us to travel not only the local Chesterfield Canal but also many smaller local rivers and taught us to be river wise.

One day there was great excitement on the canal as two "proper narrow boats" were expected. These were George and Olive Andrews "Romulus" and Ken Dunham's "Grange". These were an inspiration. They were stuck when we locals found them and we spent the remainder of the afternoon bowhauling them through the, notorious at the time, Chesterfield Canal weed. This was a turning point in my life. I had to have a Narrow Boat.

It took ten years and an enormous amount of dinghy and cruiser building and buying and selling (during which I spent my "spare" time on canal restoration all over the country) before I could at last afford to buy a "little Springer" hull. In 1978 I sold the completed Springer and purchased ex Fellows, Morton & Claytons "Jackal" (currently paired with ex FMC "Hereford") and an ambition was fulfilled. We have used Jackal for pleasure and trade and have learnt a lot ourselves, the hard way, and combined this with what we have learnt from the former full time working boaters with whom we have had the pleasure to meet.

Much of this latter in particular has never been written down. These chapters are therefore not intended to be definitive but are merely a first attempt to try and preserve something in print.

This initial effort to redress the lack of recorded information therefore not only includes my own thinking but also that of other NBOC members and friends. It is dedicated respectfully to those who have gone before and I offer them my grateful thanks.

Chapter 1. MOVING IN A STRAIGHT LINE.

This may not be as easy as it is assumed.

You have recently sold your first small boat and bought a deep draughted craft. You start off at your usual speed and suddenly the tiller develops a mind of its own and starts to push you off the counter. At the same time the boat starts to veer toward the opposite bank and, in a frantic attempt to avoid a collision, you heave valiantly on the tiller which suddenly and inexplicably goes slack, so that you have trouble not falling in the water. The boat now veers off again - this time to the other bank. At this point SLOW DOWN and I will explain what is happening before you zigzag your way to the horizon - or worse.

There are few skippers who have not experienced this; there are also few who will admit to it; but it can take (typically) months before one discovers how to steer such a boat rather than fight it. It is worth pointing out at this stage that every time you move the rudder out of a straight line you slow down imperceptibly but the accumulation of each unnecessary movement (and waste of your energy and diesel) can make the difference between keeping ahead of such notables as Arthur Bray and being overtaken by him!

It took me over a year to realise that the boat was actually trying to do its best to keep in the deeper (and hence faster) water. What one should do is *let* the tiller go over and the bows swing across for just a couple of seconds longer than common sense suggests and then straighten up with an abrupt, firm pull on the tiller when the boat is central in the channel once more. Notice that I say when the *boat* is central in the channel NOT just the bows. (Take note also that if you are really going too fast then this zigzagging will sooner or later take over regardless.)

The boat is central in the channel when what might be termed its "lateral centre of gravity" is in the centre of the channel - regardless of the position of the bows or stern. To find this centre of gravity choose a windless day and a straight bank with deep water. Push the boat sideways from the bank at various points along the side until you find one where bow and stern move simultaneously away. On the centre line of the boat across from this point is the centre of gravity. It is about a vertical line through this point that the boat will turn, although forward motion will make it appear a little further toward the bow than this. If you load or retrim your boat, the centre of gravity will of course be moved. On an unconverted motor boat it is generally a few feet forward of the engine room and on a full length conversion just near the middle. A fully laden boat is a rather a different kettle of fish and these will be discussed in a later chapter but the essential principle remains the same.

All this was equally true of your Springer - only now, with a deeper and heavier boat, it has assumed greater importance. The next problem is finding the centre of the channel. One is in it when one is steering in the direction one wants to go and the tiller lies slack in your hand. This is not always the centre of the canal. There is for example one particular bit of the Trent and Mersey Canal west of Burton on Trent where one has nearly a mile of straight canal which contains a particularly tortuous channel!

The aim then is to steam along with little more than a ripple in your wake and a finger tip touch on the tiller. If the boat starts to veer off, let her go for a moment before pulling her back into the groove and resuming your soliloquy - and see how badly everybody else does it.

The Theory

If you are not really interested in the theory of this technique then move on to the next section, otherwise here follows a bit of simple physics.

The basis of it all is that a fast flow of water implies low pressure and slow flowing or stationary water implies high pressure. The same is true of the air of course - "lows" on the weather forecast bring wind and "highs" bring settled (but not necessarily dry!) weather. As our boat initially moves through the water, water is pushed forward at the bows leaving less at the stern. Water tries to stay level and so a flow develops backwards along either side of the boat. This is known as the counter current - since it flows counter to, or in the opposite direction to, that in which we wish to travel. It has, incidentally, no connection whatever with the counter you stand on. If we are in mid channel then the counter currents on either side of the boat will be more or less equal and we remain easily there. If however we start to get too close to one side then the counter current will increase on that side and the pressure therefore **drops**. The pressure on the other side is now higher in comparison and the stern is literally pushed toward the **shallower** water. This could mean trouble but fortunately the boat actually pivots about its centre of gravity, the bows swing over and we are pointing back to deeper water. Adopting the technique described above and letting the boat go where she will, allows her to re-enter deeper water as soon as possible and she just needs straightening up when central again. Human nature though is to straighten up as soon as the bows go wrong. This worsens the counter current on the shallow side and the whole boat tends to move sideways and aground. Sometimes she can be surprisingly hard to shift!

Related to all this is the topic of bank erosion. The higher the counter current, the greater the erosive force since the fast flowing current is capable of carrying more in the way of sediment and mud from the banks. Water at the stern of the boat is once again at high pressure. There is no counter current - just a bit of turbulence - but in shallow water the abrupt change from fast flow to slow flow results in a breaking wave. Hopefully these do not follow your travels but if you should see one behind someone **else's** boat then note how still the water is by the bank just after the damaging wave has passed.

To sum up and reiterate. Fast flowing water = LOW pressure, Slow or stationary water = HIGH pressure. This means that at the bow and stern are points of high pressure (the water is literally heaped up) and the faster flowing water down the sides is of a lower pressure.

If this sounds wrong just remember that high winds are associated with LOWS on the weather map. Air and water are both FLUIDS and so this is a direct analogy.

If the change from low pressure to high pressure is not sufficiently gradual we get turbulent flow and thence storms or bank erosion!

Chapter 2. PASSING ANOTHER BOAT

Oncoming boats

As far as other boating users are concerned, passing an oncoming boat is one of the most commonly complained about ways of putting the owner of the deep draughted boat in a bad light. It is this that leads to most complaints of channel hogging and arrogance and I believe it will do a lot of good for our cause if we can find a diplomatic way of doing things.

If one meets a friend or a fellow deep draughted boat then there is no reason why you should not carry straight on at normal cruising speed toward their stem bar, only deviating from the channel when one is less than thirty feet away, and allowing the dynamics of flow around your respective hulls to carry you safely round and back into the channel as described in the previous chapter. Each boat is in effect carried round on the others counter current and, done by two experienced skippers, it is almost poetical to watch and really too quick to exchange any friendly banter.

On meeting someone without nerves of steel (iron or wood!) however, quite a different scenario needs to be enacted. The oncoming boat will usually give its character away by moving out of the centre of the channel a long way before it is really necessary. You of course cannot, otherwise you will simply swing back in off the mud some yards forward and clout the oncoming boat a resounding crash on its bows. In fact you have only a couple of realistic choices.

The first of these is to head straight on, taking as much space as you need - or as the other boat leaves (ie channel hogging) and concentrating like mad for the first sign that the other boat's bows are going to slip off the mud and hit you. This concentration (eyes veiled by the brim of your trilby and smoke trailing from your effervescent chimney!) is what is so often construed as arrogance and while the other boat sits on the mud as you pass, the near panic this can occasion in the other crew tends to inhibit any attempt at cheerful greetings.

The second choice is hassle free - all you have to do is slow down. As you do this you are able to get closer to the right of the channel than faster dynamics will allow. The fact that you are at least attempting some action will be more evident than you might think to the other boat who will probably copy, enabling you to pass by each other in only a slightly slower version of the "ideal" described above. Cheerful comments about dredgers and cups of tea will then leave all parties retreating and thinking that the world is still a wonderful place.

As your counters pass is an invigorating moment to wind the engine up again. You can then resume playing Josher flyboat captains or whatever and the other boat can start thinking what courteous people we are rather than assuming that we keep to the middle because we haven't got the nerve, or experience, to leave it.

There are of course instances where, even with a seventy foot narrow boat, you are the smaller craft of the two passing. On the larger rivers, and commercial waterways in general, be prepared to give way to large barges and other shipping. Whilst they may only regard your vessel as a nuisance, they have nevertheless undergone extensive training and passed appropriate examinations. Therefore look out for hand signals and be ready to interpret, and act upon, them and any sound signals. They will also know the channel better than you and therefore how much water you need.

Passing on the Gloucester and Sharpness Canal

Don't make the mistake of slowing down, this reduces your manoeuvrability. Immediately after passing, cross into the centre of their wake.

Overtaking

Overtaking another boat is quite a different kettle of fish. Firstly, as deeper draughted craft tend to be slower than other boats, it is very rare. Secondly it can only be done, in a confined channel, with the cooperation of the other steerer. Thirdly it takes a surprisingly long time and fourthly there is a particularly nasty danger.

Having caught up another boat do not attempt to pass unless he is aware of your intention and cooperates. People all too rarely look behind but hooting and waving is not a good way to get cooperation. Don't get closer than twenty feet (but not so far back that you seem prepared to stay there) and wait.

Whilst waiting (or even while approaching from behind) ask yourself whether you really want to pass anyway. Are you nearly at the pub/ wharf/ junction/ mooring? Is he? Are you really going that much slower behind him than you were before? Is there a particularly narrow bit of channel ahead that might slow you down again?

If you do decide to pass don't try to go too fast. If you move one mile an hour faster than the other boat (and that's probably optimistic!) it is going to take over a *minute* to get past a seventy footer and you will both be about 150 yards nearer that bridge (what bridge?) or very close to that oncoming boat that was a quarter of a mile away before.

An unavoidable effect of overtaking is that the other boat's bows will tend to swing towards you. Normally they can be avoided or at least - keeping feet clear - brushed aside but, occasionally, they may "stick" to the front of your swim, alongside the back cabin. Even with the other boat in reverse the only way out is to slow down to reduce this suction. This phenomenon is also quite common when two boats attempt to leave a broad lock without one waiting long enough for the other to get under way.

Whatever the scenario, the effects of this are frequently embarrassing if not dangerous. The leading boat will slow down, but the trailing boat may not soon enough. The result is that the leading boat tends to turn more and more across the path of the trailing boat whose bows tend to push the former's stern round even more - worsening the problem until the latter slows down.

The situation is obviously more dangerous when being overhauled by large commercial traffic. It is *essential* on commercial waterways to keep a good lookout, not only for the masts of oncoming vessels round the next bend, but also for those of craft astern. They can catch you up surprisingly quickly and, for once in common with other books on inland boat handling, I strongly recommend that you turn to face them in plenty of time, and meet them head on as described previously.

However if you cannot, keep slightly closer to them than your nearest bank and watch their wake catch up with you. Just before it reaches you turn slightly so that you head a little towards the bank and allow the first waves to hit you directly astern, ie boat and wavefront are at right angles. As soon as the vessel is past, turn hard toward mid channel and follow as close as you can along the centre line of the larger boat's wake.

Chapter 3. BENDS AND TURNS

One thing that deeper draught boats tend to have in common is larger diameter propellers. These are much more efficient than smaller, faster propellers but suffer more from what is known as the "paddle effect". The bottom blade has a more effective action than the top and this results in a tendency for the boat stern to move sideways. This is not normally noticeable in forward motion (one tends to correct automatically) but on engaging reverse the boat appears to leap sideways. If one is in open water one can put this effect to good use when turning round - providing one knows which way to go! It can also be useful when coming alongside a mooring to know whether your boat will dive neatly against the bank or away from it and accordingly how gently to reverse. Most boats (but not all) have a left hand pitch propeller (ie. viewed from the stern the propeller goes anti - clockwise in forward gear) and hence the stern will move *right* in reverse. It will be easier to come alongside a bank, and stop, on the *right* and it will be easiest to turn clockwise in open water, but easier to turn anti-clockwise in confined areas where a multi-point turn is needed as the paddle effect is most noticeable in reverse. If you don't know the direction of your pitch try it - everything will be vice versa for right hand pitch of course.

Wind and current can be friends or enemies. A boat's bows are typically further out of the water than the stern and will therefore tend to be more affected by wind. Conversely, the stern tends to be deeper in the water than the bow and is therefore more affected by water flow (or lack of it, remember). On a canal one is rarely affected by current for longer than it takes to turn a lock round, but even this is worth looking for if one is using a nearby winding hole, either use the flush itself to help you round or wait for the rebound when the surge reaches the next lock/bridge/stop narrows. The wind may seem constant to you but there can be useful eddies round even a single tree. Look for floating leaves or rubbish which show a still area away from wind or current and remember that wind blowing across a broad lock will hold you against the UPwind wall when empty but the DOWNwind wall when full. Winds can be particularly fickle in their unpredictability and have a nasty habit of blowing up river where you want to turn round. This can lead to the boat "sticking" half way (embarrassing!) and this is when "planning ahead" (if you were awake enough to do it) runs out and one is down to plain tillermanship.

Turning

As explained earlier in the chapter, a boat's rudder works by virtue of the water flowing past it. If there is no flow then there will be no effect - unless of course you are vigorous enough to *create* a flow.

In forward gear, pushing the tiller to the right will move the stern to the right. In reverse, pushing the tiller to the right will move the stern to the *left*, therefore to turn a boat anti - clockwise (with a left hand prop) one has the tiller to the right in forward gear and to the left in reverse as this will utilise the paddle effect to its best advantage. I realise of course that it is not always possible to turn in the best direction but recognition of the above should nevertheless help. I realise also that what is written in this paragraph is a simplification, what I have missed out is the most subtle point of all:-

Question, "When should you move the tiller from right to left or vice versa?"
Answer, "When you change gear of course!"

..........,WRONG!!!!!

The answer should be "As the water flow past the rudder changes direction". With modern high speed diesels with small flywheels the two answers are almost synonymous (simultaneous?) but with older slower revving engines, waiting 4 or 5 seconds if necessary can make the difference between a three-point turn and a five point turn - or even a turn at all without resorting to "sticks and string". Just in case you still haven't grasped the point, the order of events should be:-

1) Enter the turn with plenty of revs on and the tiller hard over
2) Slow engine, change gear, rev engine, PAUSE (until that critical moment when the tiller goes slack), move tiller over SMOOTHLY (but firmly)
3) Repeat (2) until facing required direction, then proceed forward.

Additionally bear in mind the following points;-

4) The turn will be tighter if started when the boat has little or no forward motion - don't go steaming up to and straight into a winding hole - slow right down (yes, even reverse!) before starting with (1)
5) Use all the space available - even if you don't think you will need it - but of course beware of other craft
6) Don't forget paddle effect, wind, tree cover, lock flushes, the butty etc.
7) Good Luck!

So far I have only been discussing directly turning round without making reference to bends or junctions but much of the above is applicable to these. Item (4) is especially applicable to junctions but I discuss bends and bridgeholes in the next chapter.

Another technique for turning is as follows. When going astern whilst turning, keep the rudder FULLY OVER but still on the ahead side. The rudder then blocks the flow to the propeller on one side causing the stern to be drawn in the correct direction. The tiller is then placed at 45 degrees to go ahead. The first technique involved putting the tiller on ALTERNATE sides at 45 degrees to go forward and astern but in both cases it is important to WAIT after changing gear before moving the tiller. This second technique is less likely to drag you off the counter (especially if the rudder blade hits an obstruction when reversing) but I think it is only really effective if you are turning in a direction which is sympathetic to the direction of the pitch of the propeller **and** your rudder will go the full 90 degrees - many modern ones in particular won't - otherwise the stern will tend to pull back sideways whence it has only just come!

Modern boaters are commonly seen using this technique and seem blissfully unaware that for every 10 degrees they turn in the desired direction in forward gear, they immediately lose nearly half when they put the engine in reverse.

Winding Holes

So far I have discussed general turning techniques, but now a brief word on these "special" places for turning round.

Firstly, it is generally agreed (although some disagree) that they are called winding holes (ie as in the blowing thing, rather than the twisting thing) because boatmen, in horse drawn days, used the wind to help blow their boats round. This is an eminently sensible thing for us, even with engine assistance, to continue to do - regardless of the origin or pronunciation of the word.

Where the hole is deep and wide enough, the techniques described previously should suffice, so all I need to add here is guidance for where they are not. As a brief aside though, the winding holes on the Bridgewater Canal are particularly large and I once derived considerable pleasure from watching, the now late Bert Dunkley, with his full length boat *Prince*, towing, the also late Joe and Rose Skinner, with their full length horse boat (strictly speaking *mule* boat) *Friendship* round a winding hole at Lymm in 1972 - without stopping!

In working days, getting the job done was a compromise between doing it as quickly as possible and expending the minimum effort. Where these two could be combined - as in using the wind - this was a considerable bonus. Also in working days, boats were either "empty" or "loaded" - none of the semi-deep draught that converted and/or fitted boats tend toward today - it was therefore not too difficult to ensure that when boats were to be winded, this was done either *before* loading or *after* unloading. This meant that even silted up winding holes were rarely a problem.

Winding *Spey* at Tamworth

On approaching a winding hole then, check which way the wind is blowing and think how it can be used to best advantage. Bear in mind in particular "Additional point 4." referred to on the previous page - followed closely by point 1. With a motor boat it is usually best to head the bows into the hole and motor the stern round. Exceptions occur when using a basin entrance, junction or other known deep water and the wind is such that it will blow the bows round for you - or you prefer to use a long shaft as in the accompanying photograph.

Sometimes it is not possible to motor the stern round as the innermost section of the hole is just too silted even for the bows. If it is an "only just/not quite" situation you can sometimes still get round by attaching a line of (say) 30 feet length to the stern and assisting the pull round with human power on the towpath. This is a good idea in any case where the possibility of objects under the water fouling the propeller is at all likely. Speaking of fouling, beware also of evidence of "dog walking" which can foul your line in quite a different way!

If even pulling round by hand fails, don't give up yet. Instead, put the *stern* into the hole as far as it will go and start to pull the bows round. You won't get very far but when you come to a sludgy stop, secure the bows to the bank and use plenty of throttle in *forward* gear. This will displace quite a lot of, usually very smelly, mud but you will then be able to reverse back further, resecure the bows and power it in forward again to displace more mud. This process of silt blasting will eventually get you round - provided the winding hole was ever big enough of course. If there is any prospect of underwater obstructions other than silt, it is probably best not to try it though - find somewhere else instead.

Notwithstanding all this the choice is yours - try the different methods yourself (in every combination). The aim behind this publication is not to be definitive but to suggest ideas and retain a variety of techniques.

Chapter 4. BENDS AND BRIDGEHOLES

In the previous section I dealt with actually turning the boat round whilst using the paddle effect of one's propeller, the wind and such current as might be available to expedite the operation. You will (hopefully !) also remember that I made a great effort to explain *when* to move the tiller in our back and forth shunting - now read on......

Traditionally, when negotiating a bend, one kept to the outside because that was where the channel should be. These days it rarely is, as modern boaters bring a motorway mentality with them which dictates that the shortest route must be taken. Due to the large numbers of these "drivers", the channel has moved at least as far as the middle. Keeping the channel to the outside has two main advantages, firstly it gives the bend a larger radius (ie less sharp) and therefore easier to get round with a longer boat. Secondly one can also see further round it and therefore find it easier to avoid someone coming the other way (assuming you haven't "blowed"!). This is especially true of waterways like the Southern Oxford where a bridge on the bend minimises the visibility anyway.

Large numbers of deep draughted, full length boats might be able to move the channel back (joke!) but trying to do it on one's own is a near impossibility and, if you are to avoid going aground repeatedly just to make a point, there is little that can be done but make a token effort and go with the flow. In the long term, re-education would be the answer but I am not optimistic. Nevertheless restating the advantages of an outside channel will do no harm whenever you get the chance.

Traditionally also, you went steaming up to bridgeholes, reduced the engine revs as the bows entered the bridge, allowed your following swell to lift the stern of the boat and then blatted off again as the engine and back cabin went through. This reduced the suction on the underwater bridge pointing, made one less likely to hit bottom and added to the general interest of boating. It also distinguished the "professional" from the "amateur". These days however there is more than a possibility of the "following swell" lifting you onto a pile of junk - and leaving you there! Rubbish in bridgeholes takes many forms necessitating different techniques for getting through. If you aren't intimately acquainted with the waterway along which you are travelling therefore I can only suggest caution ie slow down a bit sooner and more gradually. If there is an oncoming boat let it through first.

Much of what I said last time about turning a boat round is also applicable to sharp bends - especially if a bridge is involved. Take note of wind and current and slow down - almost to a stop in some cases - and then use plenty of revs to make the turn tight. If you still can't get round Sutton Stop/Hawkesbury Junction in one, then try thinking of it as two right angles instead.

Many junctions and river locks had bollards to assist unpowered craft make the turns. With the large scale introduction of powered craft many of these became redundant but can often still be seen. Some are still useful.

Taking a round turn (see section on knots) with the bow rope around the bollard is the usual way. Sometimes the "bollard" isn't what you expect though! At Hawkesbury for example, there is a hook under the bridge intended to be connected to your boats **mast**. The standard Grand Union bollard on the corner to help you enter the backwater at Abbey Park in Leicester is actually fenced off and therefore useless.

Elsewhere little bits of heritage are being lost through ignorance of their proper function - a classic example being the loss of some "holding back pins" on Grand Union Locks. These stubby little pins near the top gates are intended to take a butty rope to hold it back in the lock as the motor leaves. As outlined in the section on overtaking (leaving locks) this is actually a safety feature. Unfortunately they have also been seen as a trip hazard and there was a spate of cutting them off some years ago. Following complaints this has now hopefully stopped but just illustrates how safety matters can conflict and how doing things in the name of safety alone can create unforseen problems if done in haste and/or ignorance.

I won't go any further, in this context, than just mention hydraulic paddle gear in passing. Suffice to say that there was a declaration some years ago to the effect that no new hydraulic gear would be fitted and that existing gear would be gradually replaced with a more traditional pattern.

A pair of boats about to leave a lock. Note the butty's use of a rope on the holding back pin and the mast lines to open the gates.

Chapter 5. ON BECOMING UNSTUCK!

Coincident with the publication of the original article there were several ideas mentioned in passing in the same newsletter. In the then Chairman's column, he had to wait for the tide on the Trent to free him. Unfortunately this option is not generally available on the narrow canals!

Another option suggested was that when stuck in squidgy mud in a bridgehole you should let the boat settle in the mud first before roping through. A third suggestion was that (again in mud) you should shunt back and forwards repeatedly and thus create (dredge!) ones own trench.

In the open canal of course becoming unstuck is often a case of letting any residual momentum, combined with letting the tiller go for a moment (as described in part one) to enable the boat to slide back into the channel by herself - if she has merely gone too much to one side. Experienced steerers will however detect and correct any early imbalance of the tiller almost subconsciously in much the same way as former motorcyclists will still lean inwards on bends when driving a car! If the boat has actually come to a stop under such circumstances then reversing will generally let the boat slip bodily sideways into the channel, if it's there, or will give scope for "shunting," if it's not. The actual action of reversing sends water from behind the boat down both sides, towards the bows. Not only does this give some backwards effort but also puts some more water where you most need it and the extra water on the side nearest the bank tends to push you back to the centre of the canal if not the channel. This action can be emphasized and increased by careful use of the rudder.

The main part of this section is intended to offer help to those who have come to a halt on a pile of "something" and further use of the engine proves useless.

How to get the boat off a pile of something nasty

Rolling up on an oil drum or mattress is probably the worst, the propeller sucks air instead of water and does not "bite". Pulling on a rope from the bank or with another boat is frequently the only answer but try some of the other techniques below if these are not practical or you aren't yet desperate enough to wade to the bank!

Squidgy mud will move quite readily in a strong flow of water, so use the engine to create one IN REVERSE. Then go forward and, if she still won't go, blow some more mud away behind you to make a hole to reverse into before trying gently forwards again. If this gets you nowhere after a few go's try putting the tiller over on alternate sides on alternate tries before trying straight ahead again. The idea is to level out the mud around and under the boat. If you can get ashore it is also more sensible to use a rope to pull ahead rather than trying to do it all with the engine as, in forward gear, the stern digs deeper (or tries to). Pulling forward with the engine idling in REVERSE is particularly productive in muddy bridgeholes.

17

This levelling technique is very useful also when stuck on rubble. Using a long shaft to push the bows all the way to one side of the canal, and then the other and back again a few times, will tend to walk the boat forward if coupled with a little forward effort - of the manual kind rather than the engine kind if possible.

Rocking from side to side is another useful technique, but if overzealous can do considerable damage to internal ornaments as well as being rather alarming for 'er indoors - whoops sorry, she's not indoors of course she's controlling the engine, or on the other gunwale, or acting as ballast on the bows with the kids! - or maybe you are her and 'im's indoors? The key to rocking is to follow the *boat*'s rhythm and not try and go faster, or slower than it.

If one is stuck downstream of a lock, flushes of water from the paddles of (say) ten seconds duration can work wonders - but they can also lift you further aground if the boat is not correctly aligned, so use water carefully and combine it with some of the techniques already described, or the wrath of the Water Wizards is likely to fall on you. When actually in a lock tail, care and ropes are usually needed when flushing *in* and of course a crew member on the bank to close paddles when flushing *out!*

A pair of well crewed boats try everything!

Winches, Tirfors and blocks and tackle (I collected mine on the propeller in a bridgehole some years ago!) are potentially useful devices but their actual use is often limited by the availability of suitable things to fix the other end to. Trees are rarely in the right place and most other things tend to pull out. Those nice heavy pipes crossing the bridge are ideal for lifting the stern but not much good for pulling the bows - also beware of fracturing gas mains (or lock gates!)!

Moveable ballast - especially people gleaned from the towpath - is often sufficient in itself if you can do this readily, but avoid using "towpath youth" unless you are convinced of their moral standards. Otherwise oil drums filled with water are nearly as moveable.

If you are *still* stuck

When all is said and done of course, it is British Waterways job to keep the channel clear and so, if they fail in this respect, it is their job to remove the obstruction (and therefore you). In the few cases I have known where they have been called out, a cheery band of men in Watford Blue (then of course it became Greycaine Green, or even Red) will arrive within the hour and enthusiastically get you (but not the obstruction!) clear.

Personally I have only used this approach once.

This was after spending the night on a loaded boat under Whittington Bridge on the Coventry Canal (Birmingham and Fazeley Section) and I had nearly become paralysed from the waist down in the (November) cold water. Enough was enough. It had taken FOUR long days from Atherstone (!!!) - viz:- *First night*, Polesworth Swing Bridge. 14 hours and 2 miles later *Second night*, Pooley Hall Colliery Bridge. *Third night* (bonfire night!), Fazeley Junction. From Huddlesford Junction (where the BW sections changed) no problems all the way home.

On the morning of the fifth day therefore the Water Wizards extricated us in about an hour and even refused a cup of tea (!) but the really amazing thing was that we were the first call out (by virtue of draught - ours was a mere 2' 10" over 50 feet) that YEAR! The reason is probably that after getting ourselves unstuck we are generally so relieved that we never get around to writing that letter we were thinking about at the time.

Another problem is that if a queue develops it is YOUR BOAT that is seen as the fault rather than poor dredging. Even if you explain this to the assembled multitudes you still feel guilty.

The Non-strenuous Way

Perhaps we have done it all wrong all these years, maybe if we get stuck through no fault of our own, we should pass the buck back where it belongs and ring Freephone Canals (or Not Freephone Cellphone Canals) and just tell the assembled multitudes that the Water Wizards are coming to sort out the results of their dredging policy and leave it at that. However IF you feel public spirited enough to get yourself unstuck then don't forget to write and complain about it will you? Try starting the "Dear BW....." letter described elsewhere. Send a copy to IWAAC to help them to help us and a copy to our secretary so that we can try and get some feel for the state of the nation.

I was once speaking to a fellow club member about getting stuck. Like me he had spent many happy years boating but many unhappy hours under bridges. Finding the excitement of this beginning to pall he had adopted the policy of calling out British Waterways each time instead of struggling with tirfors and winches himself. He had received prompt and helpful attention each time and was assured that the appropriate problems would be attended to.

It used to be almost a point of honour NOT to call out BW. My own personal breaking point on this was on the journey I referred to above when we got stuck under Whittington Bridge on the Coventry Canal.

After some thought I think that it is time for a change in attitude. My reasoning is this. Firstly BW have at last begun to acknowledge that the historic craft, which are this club's "raison d'étre," are worth preserving. (One has only to think of the encouragement and incentives given to get up to sixty such craft to Braunston for the Braunston Boat Shows)

Secondly, they can't do the necessary if they don't know about the problem - we all think up marvellous letters when boating but which we never get round to sending after becoming unstuck. Anyway, a letter *after* the event means that you managed to get through in the end unassisted, doesn't it ?

Thirdly, all the calls go through one security office which should make real problems more obvious. All calls are logged and the Board aim to meet every call within three hours.

Especially now that we are seen as "customers" it should be a lot easier to get the Board to keep to their statutory (ie. Transport Act) obligations where it comes to more dredging rather than spending more money on unnecessary new signs, picnic tables etc. for those who don't pay directly for their upkeep.

Customer Care means more dredging, less dressing!
(Gosh, another "T" shirt slogan!)

So next time you get REALLY (as opposed to marginally - joke!) stuck try ringing Freephone Canals (or 01384 215785 the special NBOC or "Narrow Boats On Cellnet" number) and see if it's really worth all that sweat.

Chapter 6. MOVABLE BRIDGES ETC.

These can be a pig, but for the moment let's assume the bridge will work smoothly. If you have a crew of two or more there should be no problem either and so much of what follows is directed toward the single hander. Whether lift bridge or swing, the pivot is almost invariably on the opposite bank to the towpath. The reason for this is so that the horse will not have to stop to clear the towline........ Wait!....... What horse?... Precisely! and, at the risk of being shouted down as a non- traditionalist, why do we perpetuate this reasoning, except in habit, when bridges are replaced? On the other hand, I would not like them on the towpath side if I ever had to bowhaul through them...... but I digress.

Bridges of all types tend to have more than their fair share of rubbish beneath them so avoid either bank on approaching the bridge and put your bows against the wall inside the bridge narrows themselves on the off (ie. non-towpath/pivot) side. The chances of a bollard being to hand are within three decimal places of nil, so use a simple knot (see later, section 7) to tie the bow rope loosely to some immovable object or, if trees and thistles won't oblige, use the bridge railings but remember that they aren't designed for it so tie the rope as low as possible to minimise the effects of leverage. The next job is to get on the bank in the appropriate place to operate the bridge. The offside typically has some vicious nettles and brambles, so climb over the bridge railings themselves. Remember that road traffic will not be expecting your abrupt materialisation and, if you have been boating for more than a few days, you will have forgotten just how fast cars can go!

If it's a push button bridge make sure your boat (and the traffic) is sufficiently clear and push the buttons following the instructions, or your instincts, as the case may be. If it's a manually operated bridge continue as below.

Lift bridges

As well as being the easiest to work (usually!) they are also the most dangerous and fatalities do occur. Remember this and do not be tempted to trust their operation to groups of small boys and the like. Similarly NEVER put yourself in a position where, if the bridge did fall, it could hit you and/or squash you against any immovable object (and I include the boat in this). In other words if you have to duck, DON'T lean forward over the cabin but crouch down in the space between the cabin and the tiller. Don't lean over that either.

Some lift bridges are operated by hydraulic paddle type gearing, but many of these have been replaced fairly rapidly as the adjustment seems to be rather critical. More common are wire or chain winch mechanisms which seem to be fairly reliable and don't require further comment from me. This leaves us with the balance beam type which can be either high level (eg. Caldon or Llangollen Canals) or low level (eg, Southern Oxford).

Both these types are designed to toggle from the open to closed positions. Ie. they should be stable in either position and to move them from either position should require some effort. (NB the wind can do this unexpectedly sometimes). All too frequently balance weights have been removed or the pivot suffers from age or is jammed by stones. I usually take a rope or even a mud weight onto the bank with me to fix the balance beam in the open position. This is not always possible and, if the bridge really doesn't want to stay open, we have to resort to, the "Banbury Stick".

This is quite a different technique and, as its name suggests, devolves from the Southern Oxford Canal. Uniquely it involves getting off the boat on the *towpath*, or non-pivot, side. The bridge is then levered, or lifted by the railings, to a height where the stick can be jammed between the edge of the underside of the bridge and the edge of the bank. Note: It is quite easy at this point to fall through the gap.

The stick itself can be any sort of bit of wood about 3 feet (1m) long. I use a short gang plank with a slight "V" or curve at either end to inhibit slipping but your (almost obsolete) Calder and Hebble handspike or similar is probably more traditional. Rather than merely passing through, and then having to stop again to retrieve the "stick", the old boatman's technique included a short line attached to the base of the stick to pull it out (without stopping of course) after passing through. The bridge would, under the influence of gravity, return to its closed position with a gentle thud (sic).

Getting stuck under a lift bridge is a distinctly unnerving experience and I will merely refer you to the previous section and the warnings at the start of this one.

Swing Bridges

Although inherently safer than lift bridges the balancing is even more critical and so swing bridges almost invariably stick somewhere. Usually the discreet addition of part of one's own body weight at one point or another is sufficient to dislodge them. Only rarely and in extreme cases will the use of a lever (Banbury Stick perhaps?) be necessary.

Care is needed. There is a risk that the whole bridge can be unshipped and BW will not be amused by damage caused by unnecessary force on swing or lift bridges and could well send you a bill. Arguing that it should have been better maintained is unlikely to get you anywhere. The correct procedure of course, is to always call out BW when a problem in excess of a reasonable nature is encountered, regardless of the circumstances.

On regularly used waterways the bridges are swung frequently but people forget this too easily and tend to resort to unnecessarily violent means on bridges that really don't deserve it. Almost invariably it is technique that is wrong - ie misdirected effort - rather than the bridge itself. Perfectly good, delicately balanced bridges have been damaged by such abuse.

The first thing to do with a bridge that doesn't respond easily is to check that there aren't any locking devices (such as flip over hinged bars or links to adjacent fences) that you have missed. Next, see if you can make the bridge rock. You should be able to make the bridge balance with your own mass, so that another crew member can push it easily. This technique can be much quicker than trying to force a bridge which catches on all the adjacent masonry.

Nudging an awkward bridge with a boat is a fairly brutal way to do things. Attaching a rope to the *base* of a handrail support on the opposite side of the pivot and pulling with the boat removes much of the shock. The use of a suitable slip knot will then enable you to go forwards through the bridge without stopping. Taking a long line from a stern dolly around the furthest three sides of the bridge, round a handrail stanchion and all the way back again will enable you to pull the bridge closed behind you. Release one end of the line and pull in on the other as you sail into the distance. Confused? .... then don't try it but whatever you try, attach ropes as close as possible to the bridge platform to minimise strain. Remember also that if it goes wrong YOU are responsible and that an audience ALWAYS appears at those embarrassing moments!

Chapter 7. KNOTS AND MOORINGS
Knots

I don't expect, as elsewhere, the following to be definitive and nor will I bore you with repetitions of the clove hitches, bowlines and eye and back splices with which I expect you to be already familiar - or at least which appear in almost every practical boating book or knot book. Instead, it is my intention to reveal some simple, useful, but unusual, knots and some unusual uses for simple, usual knots. Try saying that in a hurry!

Regrettably I have to further preface this with some definitions so that you know what I'm talking about but, in the interests of simplicity, they aren't "official" definitions either.

A KNOT is a fastening in rope or cord and will probably be either a BEND (ie joining two ropes or similar) or a HITCH (ie joining a rope to a ring, pole, bollard etc). A few knots (such as bowlines) fall in to neither category.

A BIGHT is either the bit of a rope *where* you are tying the knot (as distinct from the END *with* which you usually tie it) or is a loop or curve formed in the rope. The main part of the rope (ie the opposite side of a bight to the end) is called the STANDING PART.

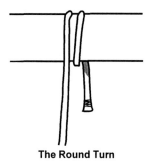

The Round Turn

I shall start with **THE ROUND TURN** - not a knot in itself but very useful and very important. Note in particular that the rope goes *at least* one complete turn round the spar (or it might be a bollard) and the resulting friction means that only very slight tension is required at the end to hold a very heavy load (or boat!) on the standing part. Relaxing this slight tension enables controlled release of the load - ideal for slowing down a boat or gate strapping. Note however that an extra turn is not only unnecessary but will possibly jam - ideal for breaking ropes when gate strapping!

The round turn - when used as a fastening - usually has two half-hitches to complete it, but an interesting variation is the **ANCHOR HITCH or FISHERMAN'S BEND** where the rope end is first passed through the coils of the round turn before being whipped or half-hitched to the standing part. This is an extremely strong and reliable knot which won't fall undone. Use it to fasten anchor ropes to chains rather than directly to the anchor though.

There seems to be some disagreement on the correct way to tie the Fisherman's Bend however. Some authorities suggest that I have put my second half hitch the wrong way round - the argument being that the way I have shown it, the two half

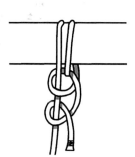

The Anchor Hitch

24

hitches would form a clove hitch (see elsewhere) around the standing part and could jam - although, ironically, this would be quite correct for a round turn and two half hitches.

In the half dozen or so books to which I and others have referred, the opinion is equally divided. The oldest version - from a sixty year old seaman's manual - shows the second half hitch the other way. My oldest personal reference was a book published in the year of my own birth (coincidentally) and does not therefore quite have the precedence of the other but this is the version shown as it appeared in the original article. It is interesting to note that the alternative version results in a **LARK'S HEAD KNOT**. (see below) around the standing part. In truth I suspect it doesn't actually matter as some versions of the knot do not even show a second half hitch and, either leave the end free or, suggest whipping it to the standing part for neatness.

Marline Spike Hitch

The **MARLINE SPIKE HITCH** is a very simple knot formed by making a twist in a section of rope with one hand and pulling a bight, from the standing part, through the loop with the other hand. Traditionally a Marline Spike (metal, conical tool used in ropework - the wooden equivalent is a FID) was then passed behind the section of standing part and over the loop and could be used as an aid to pulling on the rope. Quite apart from its possibilities in manual towage it is ideal to slip over a bollard as it is strong out of all proportion to its simplicity and can be tied and applied in less than five seconds. Use it therefore when working locks and for holding the lines while you operate a movable bridge.

A better known alternative is the **LARK'S HEAD KNOT or COW HITCH**. Again it is very simply formed on a bight or at the end of a rope with a loop (it is actually intended to have equal strain on both ends). I use this for fastening ropes to the masts and to dollies (ie used with an eye splice). I do not personally use it for tying up (although many do) as I find the marline spike hitch easier to undo and adjust.

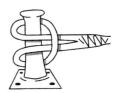
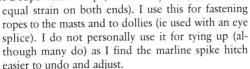

Lark's Head Knot

Catspaw

In an enlarged form the Lark's Head Knot becomes the **BARREL SLING** (not illustrated) and if both loops are first twisted fully round in opposite directions and then placed over (eg) a hook it becomes the **CATSPAW** which cannot jam. In some books it is used as a means of shortening a sling - in mine merely to provide a non-jamming attachment of a sling to a hook - in non-critical applications I might add!.

A simpler knot to attach to a hook is the **BLACKWALL HITCH** This is only safe under tension and I include it mainly because it is the knot to use for long- (or thumb-) lining when opening the gates from the boat while descending a lock.

Blackwall Hitch

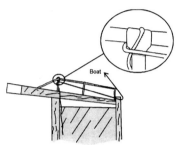

Thumb lining

T**HUMB LINING.**
Contemporary handrails tend to be thinner than they used to be and the knot tends to slip. Counteract this by spiralling the free end ONCE round the vertical stanchion at the top of which you have tied the knot (closest to the heel post) and take the standing part diagonally downwards and round the mitre or breast post of the gate back to the boat - definitely NOT the top of the handrail end or you may rip it off. Done correctly there is no chance of damage resulting (for which I am sure BW would successfully sue - in spite of your protestations about rotten gates) and my main purpose for including this item is so that this technique is used CORRECTLY, rather than ineptly without prior knowledge. Preferably let someone show you but if you intend to be adventurous then practise it manually first with a long rope and no boat. (See also photograph, page 16)

F or a quick release knot use the **COWBOY or HIGHWAYMAN'S HITCH.** Form a bight about three feet (say 1m) from the end of your rope and pass this behind the rail/ ring/ bollard. Form a second bight in the standing part, pass this over the rail etc. and through the first bight. Form a third bight in the free end and pass through the second bight. The standing part will now hold your horse (or boat) quite happily, but a firm pull on the free end will undo the lot.

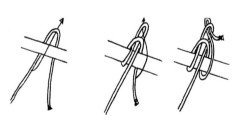

Cowboy or Highwayman Hitch

26

Next, the **HALF SHEEPSHANK**. This is commonly used as a primitive block and tackle, although friction reduces the theoretical maximum mechanical advantage of two down to about one and a half. Some boaters (and nowadays lorry drivers) have used it for tying ropes tightly over cloths. An extra twist in the loop "X" before passing the end through will reduce any tendency for the thing to come undone.

Half Sheep- shank

The **SLIPPERY HITCH** - this is essentially the same as the Blackwall Hitch except that a bight rather than the end is tucked under the standing part. This is really handy when going down narrow locks single - handed as it can be applied to a strapping post on a short rope from the bows while the lock fills to save a lot of awkward running up and down and on and off the boat. After opening the gate, by reversing away, the hitch should fall off as the boat enters.

Slippery Hitch

The **WEST COUNTRY WHIPPING** is probably the simplest and most reliable of all whippings for natural fibre rope ends although it lacks the tidiness of some. It is merely a succession of "left over right and unders" tied alternately front and back, moving away from the rope's end. Tie each part as close together as possible. The sections are shown separated here for clarity. Finish it with a reef knot.

West Country Whipping

The **FIGURE OF EIGHT KNOT** is self descriptive and can be used as a stopper knot on a rope's end (a) or on a "T" stud (b). Contrary to what some writers will have you believe it was sometimes used in this way by working boaters as photographs give evidence. The trick to avoiding

(a)   (b)   (c)

Figure of Eight Knot

it jamming (the reason for its supposed lack of favour) is to carry the standing part BEHIND the upright of the "T" and then form a WHOLE figure of eight before tucking the end away. There is then negligible strain on the end which can be easily unlocked.

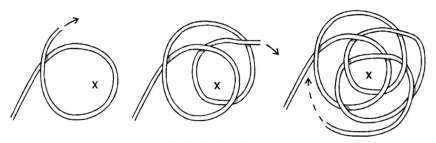

The Turk's Head Knot

The **TURK'S HEAD KNOT or PASHA'S NAPPA** is actually a very straightforward knot (stage 2 is merely a clove hitch) and the version shown is ideal to slip over a tiller or shaft etc before going round the whole thing again twice more. This is where particular care is needed to follow exactly the previous line and not divert on to the wrong strand or cross over one. Get the initial knot and each subsequent follow round tidy before proceeding. Take care also when going round for the final tightening as it is still quite easy to mess the whole thing up at the last post. For special purposes you may have to increase the number of ins and outs but this I leave to you with the exception of one example. This I call (for descriptive purposes only) the Long Turk's Head.

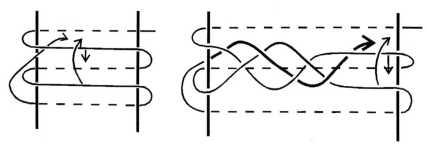

The "long" Turk's Head Knot

The *"Long"* **TURK'S HEAD**, for the butty ram's head, is rather special. This is difficult to show in a drawing, but the idea is that, having formed a simple spiral first, in a very long loop, a bight from one of the side strands is passed across and the free end woven through it. This is then repeated to create as many bights as required. The whole thing is best done off the boat. I did ours on a pair of oars held about 10" apart and then stretched the completed article onto the ram's head.

Finally ONE way of tying over the cloths. You need enough rope to go from the edge of one side cloth over the top plank to the other cloth THREE times (i.e. 10 - 12 feet) or for top cloths you need rope to go from one gunwale over the top plank to the other gunwale THREE times (about 25 feet). With one end eye spliced on to the appropriate eye or ring, take the free end over the top, through the other eye or ring and back over the top plank. Pull tight. Make a round turn (see chapter 7 - first knot) under the standing part, carry the end back over the top plank and make another round turn. Finish by passing the end between the two strands here and then spiralling down around them before tucking through again.

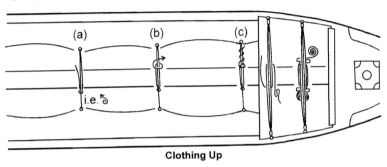

Clothing Up

The rope work for the cratch is similar but you start with a separate rope, spliced to each side, and you handle the two simultaneously. The ends are first taken through the opposite splice, back over the top and under the opposite strands, back across the top and tucked with an "S" and a spiral... Got that?

You should end up with three strands each side and six over the top but there are other ways.

On the subject of cratch decoration, whilst at the local fire station (getting advice on boat fire extinguishers) I asked if they had any spare canvas fire hose to replace that which was showing signs of age across *Jackal's* cratch. After they had stopped laughing I found out that it hadn't been used for many years but I was welcome to some offcuts of the new pvc red stuff. Declining this offer, I went to a Real Army Surplus store where I found a particularly awful length of old hose for an exorbitant price but, before purchasing this, I spotted a reel of white, glass fibre webbing - apparently ideal for the purpose. It didn't need whitening and shouldn't rot. I also used some for lagging the exhaust and repairing the dinghy!

The alternative for the cratch, is to buy a length of "webbing" from your rope supplier or tarpauliner.

Moorings

Full length and/or deep draughted boats tend to experience more problems mooring up than one might expect. Owners of boats in the thirty to fifty foot bracket commonly see a space as just a space. Only the owner of a seventy-ish foot boat has to consider not only whether the space available is long enough but also whether it is *straight* enough so that the ends or middle of his craft will not stick out and obstruct the channel too much. Only the owner of the deep draughted boat will also worry whether that inviting section of bank is *deep* enough for him and his boat (or even his gangplank) to reach the side.

As any experienced boater will tell you, the oft quoted advice in many cruising guides along the lines of "…bringing your craft parallel with and gently alongside the bank" usually results in you screeching to a halt on a pile of submerged bricks so that the bank is *just* out of reach and your propeller froths impotently under the counter. No thank you!

Better safe than sorry, approach the bank at quite a sharp angle with the intention of bringing the bows to a halt at the edge of the bank for a crew member to take a rope ashore. Do however take the cruising guides advice and don't allow a crew member to teeter on the extreme stem ready to leap ashore at the earliest possible moment. This is dangerous as, if you run aground at this moment, they will be catapulted into the water or onto the bank. The resulting crumpled and/or soggy heaps are fairly common near hire boat bases in the Spring. Most escape injury but…

If you do run aground at this point, judicious use of a short shaft should tell you whether it's an obstacle you can remove, moor next to, or whether you will have to try elsewhere.

Having found a suitably long and deep enough site, we come to the moment when we can actually tie up. Nevertheless, don't stop the engine until the boat is secure. Conversely, never untie until the engine is running. A drifting boat - whether in wind or current - is a liability. I once saw a hire narrow boat drift into and damage two cruisers on the Trent just because everyone expected the engine to start *"next* time" and the crew simply didn't bother to take avoiding action even though this would have been easy, right up to the moment of impact, using the ropes they still had in their hands at the time. Sadly *I* expected the engine to start "next time" as well and so didn't bother to shout a warning.

Working single handed, it is a useful idea to trail the bow rope along the cabin top or top plank, as the case may be, so that you can more easily jump ashore with it, without having to walk the whole length of the gunwales to collect it. The "back end line" (ie from the rear of the *hold* remember) is a usable alternative in the initial attempt to get the boat to the bank but beware that the bows don't swing out and you are left with a gap of six feet of water to cross because the boat won't come any closer! With even one crew member the job is obviously much simpler - especially in windy conditions or where there is a flow to contend with.

Another warning at this point is to ensure that if either of your bow or back end ropes fall or blow overboard that they are not long enough to reach the "blades". Your stern line should normally be carried, detached, on the cabin top within reach of the steerer, neatly coiled and ready for any immediate use. *Never* hang it over the tiller pin - not only is this untidy but the whole lot may well end up in the water. If you need longer ropes than suggested above for certain rivers etc then these should be hanked up well out of the way until needed.

Tying up

A rmed with the section on knots above, and what you may have gleaned from elsewhere, you will have hopefully mastered all the knots you need to tie your boat up. As with so many things though, knowledge of the facts is not enough, the way you do it can also be important. A certain well known waterway personality reputedly once tied up a dredger on a large river. In flood. To a *Thistle*! I would not recommend this but it does demonstrate what can be achieved when technique is added to a mere knot. What you do however is largely dictated by the type of bank to which you tie and the depth of water you find there.

Wash from speeding craft is often given as the reason for mooring spikes being pulled out and boats going adrift. This is not strictly accurate. Wash from a speeding craft will try to make your boat move with it (as will the water movement from a nearby lock) and it is the momentum of *your own boat* that then pulls out the spikes. Mere up and down motion is unlikely to do this, it is the *back and forward* motion that we must minimise. Even a succession of non-speeding craft can gradually create more and more slack in the ropes so that the boat will eventually end up adrift.

Amongst the narrow boat fraternity, it must be said, a rope was never a rope but a **STRAP**. We thus had fore-end straps, short straps, cross straps and so on. I must admit that I only regularly use the latter of these terms, and tend to use "rope" and "line" interchangeably to make myself more easily understood. It could be argued that I am therefore guilty of demeaning the tradition I try so desperately to keep alive in these pages. Forced to plead guilty to this charge I can only promise to try harder in future.

What to tie where

H opefully I am preaching to the converted in this section, but for completeness in this publication, I will reiterate what I expect you already know.

Let us assume for the moment that you are able to get close to the bank and are merely intending to tie with a strap at the bow and another at the stern. An increasingly common fault is to take the ropes at right angles from the boat to the bank. Even worse, some take the ropes at an angle towards the middle section of the boat. The first of these options doesn't stop forward or backward motion and the second emphasizes it by making the boat swing round an imaginary pivot somewhere at the back of the towpath hedge.

What you should do is take the bow rope *forward* at about 45° and, similarly, the stern rope *aft* at about 45°. Not only does this minimise fore/aft movement but also simultaneously minimises sideways movement. This is something of a compromise, but one which copes with most mooring situations. Don't worry if these ropes cross those of a neighbour. Some people consider this an infringement of their "personal space" but it is surely better to do this than risk constant bumping of your boat with theirs. Indeed, tying neighbouring stem and stern posts together will make you virtually impervious to the effects of passing craft.

If you are unable to get close to the side at all, then tie the ropes even further along the bank, away from the ends of the boat, and change the angle so that each line becomes more and more parallel to the bank. In the extreme, if your boat is eight or ten feet away from the bank, you may well need bow and stern ropes twenty five or thirty feet long. These ropes will no longer be sufficient however to stop you *yawing*, ie twisting about the mid point of the boat. This is not a problem in itself but it does encourage the boat to work its way onto or through the mud toward the bank, thereby slackening the ropes and making it more likely for your mooring pins to be pulled out. To stop this we need to use one or more *springs*. These are additional ropes taken diagonally once again, but in the opposite direction to the main mooring ropes - similar to those in the following diagram. Ideally, you would use one at either end of the boat but I find that a single spring taken forward from the back end rail is usually sufficient. Alternatively a single spring taken *aft* from the mast or even bow stud will suffice if the bows are close to the bank, as below. In extreme circumstances you may also need one or two more ropes (ie six in all), known as breast ropes, which go at right angles to boat and bank and prevent bow or stern going away sideways.

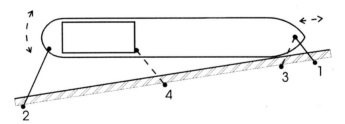

Mooring to a shallow bank

A common situation though is as shown above, where the bows can be got close to the bank but the stern cannot. Usually ropes 1 and 2 are sufficient, as previously described, but movement is still possible in the directions shown by the dotted arrows. Counteract this with rope 3 and, if necessary, rope 4 from either the back end rail or the stern itself. There is a temptation to use the *same* rope for 1 and 3. There is nothing wrong with this in principle but it is important to *tie* the rope at *all* points, rather than just looping round. Otherwise, the rope will simply work back and forth round the fixing and negate much of the good it is supposed to have done.

The use of all these ropes will rarely be necessary. If you are just fetching a pint of milk from the shop over the bridge you will probably just use the engine room line tied loosely through a ring or piece of fence, but if you are leaving the boat for a few days, they should help you sleep easier in your bed elsewhere.

Mooring Pins and Fenders

Six ropes will probably require six mooring pins. Experience has shown that a full length ex-working narrow boat requires pins between thirty and thirty six inches in length and about an inch in diameter. Most chandlers don't sell this sort of hardware as the relatively lightweight modern boat doesn't need it. Mine have been acquired from scrap heaps over the years - including the burnt out remains of an ancient Nottingham tram - but probably the next cheapest source is offcuts from reinforcing bars (hunt out the foreman at your nearest civil engineering project) or offcuts from tie bars on bank protection (see your local BW foreman). Add some semblance of a point with an angle grinder and drive them into the ground, 2-3 feet (0.6-1m) from the water's edge and to within about eight inches (0.2m) of the surface. They should be driven at about 15° to the vertical and pointing *away* from the tying point on the boat. This minimises the chance of their pulling out.

I always try, for security reasons, to tie rope ends back on the boat. I do not simply take a round turn around the pin but usually incorporate a clove hitch so that if the pin is pulled out it will remain attached to the rope rather than getting lost. This also means that any passing good samaritan only has to hammer it back in again in my absence. All attachments to mooring pins should be pushed as close to the ground as possible to reduce the effects of leverage. Placing a protective cap (eg sawn off washing up liquid bottle) over the protruding end of the pin may save your shins, or those of your neighbour, from a nasty gash but painting the ends of the pins white is arguably just as effective and probably tidier.

To remove the pins I usually give an abrupt pull sideways in both directions before pulling directly out. Only if this fails do I resort to a hammer blow to each of the four winds. I've never been forced to leave one behind yet although I did once forget to pick up one of my "tram bars" from the embankment at Nantwich.

To leave the mooring, give the bows a good push away from the side before walking along the bank or gunwale and pushing off the stern. Although I occasionally wish for a bow thruster in particularly adverse conditions, I would never use one just to get away from the bank. I suspect their increasing use for this purpose will prove very detrimental to fragile banks over a number of years.

Apart from the obvious use of ropes and mooring spikes or rings or bollards, some people use two short lengths of chain when mooring adjacent to piling. These each have a round ring in one end and an elongated ring in the other (and are incidentally used in proprietary materials handling). The elongated ring is passed under a convenient tie bar behind the piling and then through the round ring before being attached to the boat by a rope in your normal way.

Some evidence suggests there is also a need for fenders (at least 4½" or 115mm in diameter) when tying against steel piling because of the risk of worsening electrolysis in the long term. The chemical release by many concretes is also a good argument for fenders when mooring against such banks.

On the subject of cathodic protection it has been suggested in the past, that iron hulls should not need protection except for (zinc) anodes either side of the propeller tube, to which the shaft should be connected via copper brushes. I would add that iron hulls with attached steel bits (eg. new bottoms and footings) should have anodes on the STEEL as this will corrode marginally ahead of the iron. Modern thinking is that magnesium anodes should be used in preference to zinc on inland waters. The more you use, the better is the protection *and* the slower they dissolve, but the number of possible locations is somewhat limited by the need to avoid scraping them off around locks and other underwater structures.

Chapter 8. LOCKS

Although much of what has gone before is equally applicable to the novice boater, this section in particular is aimed at those who already have a modicum of boating experience - mainly in order to keep this publication to a readable length. The innumerable little ways for getting through these devices developed over the two centuries of "modern" navigation would defy the best memory in the world. This is just an attempt to save some of these gems for posterity instead of lamenting the lack of their use or their passing.

Locks: Going Uphill - Basics

On approaching a lock (and we will assume it is unmanned, self operated etc) if the gates are open and it is obviously unoccupied then of course you can enter and get on with the rest of the operation. If you come to a halt on a pile of silt or rubble then this is a different problem (see below) but normally you will arrive at a lock with all gates closed and no one around. First let us assume we are going UP. I will also assume that you are working single handed as this is the most difficult option.

With a narrow lock and a single boat it is common practice to take the boat right up to the gates, contacting them with as little force as possible, before leaving the boat ticking over in forward gear and stepping off to empty the lock. It is a fine line between "touching" the gates though and "hitting" them - which is obviously unacceptable. Once empty, the boat will nose her own way into the lock, giving you the chance to step back on and take her up to stop at the top sill. Leaving her in gear as before, climb onto the cabin top and up the lockside to close the bottom gates and raise the top paddles.

When winding the first ground paddle, stop when it's half way up and count five seconds before finishing the job. The first flush pushes the boat back and the second reduces the abruptness with which she reconnects with the top gate. When full, as the top gate starts to open, leave the beam and step across the gap which is opening to close the far paddle. As the boat is leaving the lock step back across her stern to close the rest of the paddles. As the stern passes over the sill, change her from forward to reverse gear (still at only tick over or a little above) and pull the gate shut. At this point the boat will be almost stationary at the head of the lock enabling you to step on and steam onward.

Problems

That is how it should be. Now let's take a look at what can go wrong. Firstly the lower gates may not open fully. Repeated opening and shutting will loosen silt and many obstructions but otherwise a long shaft will probably do the job. If even this fails someone may have to go in the water - be friendly toward British Waterway staff, you never know when you may need them!

Secondly, the boat may go aground before you are fully in the lock. Silt from the bywash is a frequent cause and if all the rocking, bursts from the engine in alternate forward and reverse gears, pulling in on ropes etc does not free the boat easily, then you could try a short flush from the top paddles if the boat is part in, or from the bottom paddles if you haven't managed to reach the gates yet, but before doing so, tie a rope from the bows tightly to the top of the mitre post on the gate with the gate shut and then try and open the gate. The idea is to use the whole gate as a lever with the heel post as the fulcrum. In this case you could still flush from the top paddles as long as you are able to stop the bottom gates slamming shut The main problem of flushing with any gates open is the danger of washing rubbish against the sill, so avoid it wherever possible.

The actual flushing consists of raising paddles on both sides of the lock as rapidly as possible and then closing them after about ten seconds. In the first instance leave the boat in neutral and try and flush backwards to go for a second or third run. Otherwise, the boat is best left in forward gear on a fast tick over. Her bows will rise initially and then fall as the flush ends. Nothing may appear to happen for a few seconds so don't rush into a second flush straight away. If you look carefully you should see the wave you have created disappearing down the pound. If it rebounds off another, lower lock or bridge narrows then this reflected wave is the one to do the real good but even a straight length of canal will have some effect. Flush and wait.

Thirdly, the difference in height between the top of the boat and the lock coping may require a small ladder or specially adapted gang plank but make sure there is a stable place to stand it. Many former working boat crews had a special mat on the roof for jumping on. Alternatively, bits of string, or even radio, may be able to control the boat for you!

If the lock has a suitable bollard (and the deeper ones do tend to be better provided with them) then check the boat's progress into the lock using an appropriate rope rather than all that gear changing and engine fiddling. This also saves climbing on and off the boat an extra time.

Fourthly, the lock may not fill properly (I assume you have already checked that bottom paddles are fully down and gates properly shut and that you have *all* the upper paddles open). The most common leaks are between bottom gates and poking a long shaft or gang plank down the upstream side of the gap will generally help. Only as a last resort, give the top gate a gentle nudge and put the end of a piece of timber in the gap. A Calder and Hebble handspike (3"x2") is ideal. Fingers and feet can be crushed out of all recognition so beware. Incidentally, report all such navigational problems to BW **in writing**.

I suggest you start a "Dear BW....." letter at the start of the trip and add bits as you go along. If you find nothing wrong use the letter to write and congratulate them!

The next most likely thing to go wrong is mis-timing the boat leaving the head of the lock but if you have done as I suggested and left her in reverse then she will at least come back for you.

Finally, take great care - especially on your own. Watch out for slimy green coping stones and keep all valued appendages well out of harm's way.

The situation with broad locks is slightly different. If you take a single boat up to the bottom gates she will tend to thrash dramatically from side to side unless you hold her with a rope - which defeats the object of going up to the gates in the first place. Even with a pair of boats the suckdown of a full lock emptying tends to stick bows under beams except in the very few cases where there is some protective planking. The safest option is therefore to use the bollards when you can. Unless you can get the whole boat to the bank however, only tie the bows and keep the stern away otherwise the flush may land it on the bottom.

Once in the lock the traditional way is to use a centre, back end or a bow rope and to keep the boat to the side (no trouble with two boats - but if they are of different lengths ensure that the bows, not the sterns, stay level). The only problem with this is that if the bows do decide to swing over one has to put up with more of the thrashing about mentioned earlier. My own preference is therefore to use a bow rope and push the tiller so that the stern moves to the opposite side and the boat lies diagonally. Tiller strings (see page 42) are invaluable here. This results in even less bumping than using bow and stern ropes. Grand Union locks are more gentle than some other broad locks (eg on the eastern Trent and Mersey) and a centre or "back end" line may be sufficient.

Leaving the lock is similar to leaving a narrow lock but with two boats it helps if both boats hold back at the head of the lock while the gates are shut.

There is also the non engine version of lock working. It is quite common to see a boat pulled out of the lock on a rope and this works perfectly well once the boat is moving but is not so easy to stop it! A little used way to get the boat moving easily is to tie the bow rope to a convenient point on the gate as the lock fills the last few inches or pass a turn round the strapping post. If the line is tight enough then you can open the gate *and* start the boat moving at the same time using the extra leverage provided by the balance beam. The same technique could be used to get the boat moving *into* the tail of the lock - especially if stuck, as described before.

Locks: Going Downhill - Basics

As previously, if you are approaching a narrow lock, the top gate is open and it is obviously unmanned, then sail straight in either:-

(a) putting her in reverse as the engine room passes the gates (the number of revs of course depend on your forward momentum!), then stepping off the counter to close the top gate so that you can then step back on the boat and put her in neutral, just as the boat comes to a **silent** (ie negligible speed) halt against the bottom gates. Or :-

(b) leaving her moving forward into the lock, take a short line off the counter with you - one end of which is **securely** attached to the **offside** dolly and use the strapping post on the gate, as previously described, to stop the boat and close the gate simultaneously. Don't risk doing this if there is **anyone** near the balance beam as they won't be expecting it to move. Neither should you adopt this technique in a way where you might pull a handrail off a gate. Pulling a handrail **onto** a gate (ie working the same way the bolts do rather than trying to stretch them) is quite a different matter.

By far the best way to learn is to get someone to show you - just remember that to do it wrongly is not only dangerous but could render you liable for any damage caused.

The strapping technique has largely died out - not just because of the reduction in strapping posts, but because most modern boats are simply not heavy enough.

Having got into the lock, with gate and paddles fully shut behind you, opinions differ on whether the engine should be left in gear with the bows between the breast posts of the bottom gates or left in neutral. Beware however that the bows do not catch on the tops of the mitres. Leaving it in gear theoretically means that you can open the bottom gates when the lock is empty and the boat will come out by herself while you wind the paddles down, steeping nimbly (!) across the roof to get from one side to the other. On locks with bridges across the tail you have usually even got time to close the gates and run round the other side of the bridge to leap on the counter before the boat does a "Marie Celeste" down the pound - but check out the ground first.

The usual alternative, leaving the boat in neutral, means you have to open gates, wind paddles down, climb down onto the boat, engage forward gear then either climb up again to close the gates or poke them shut with a short shaft on the end of the beam (not easy on steel ones).

Problems

Firstly, the top gate will probably be shut. If the lock is obviously completely full, then simply put the bows to the bank just short of the gate, take a precautionary rope with you, open the gate and manually pull the boat in - it's a lot quicker and safer than climbing back on, gunwale trotting seventy odd feet and using the engine. More usually, the lock will require some filling, so take the bows right up to the gate before proceeding similarly - pushing the boat manually away from the gate when full. Big Grand Union boats need to take particular care that their bows do not demolish some of the more "accessible" ground paddle posts if the boat slews diagonally while the lock is filling.

Unless you really know the area do NOT take ANYONE'S advice to go alongside the bank while the lock fills - in spite of attractive looking new bollards etc.. Filling the lock takes water out of the pound you are in. On short pounds this can mean **inches** and you may get horribly stuck. Even on long pounds it can cause embarrassment. In windy weather I use a rope or a short shaft/gangplank (depending on wind direction) to keep the stern away from the side.

When descending the lock, even with the boat in gear, the bows may disengage from the "V" between the bottom gates and unless you have taken the precaution of having a suitable rope on the bank to relocate them it can mean you having to

Waiting for a Nene Lock to fill - note the rope round the bollard and the boat away from the gates and bank.

get back on the boat to reverse it, to open the gates, to get the boat out etc etc etc. In an ideal world a handy bollard on the lockside will enable you to keep the bows clear of the bottom gates while still enabling you to clear the cill at the other end. (A handy bollard would of course enable you keep the bows clear of the gate before entering - but such things are rare.)

This is perhaps a good time to remind you not to engage in too much idle chatter whilst working a lock. Even when there are no paddles to wind or gates to move, you should constantly **watch the boat** to ensure that she ascends or descends smoothly and does not catch anywhere - be ready to drop paddles in an emergency. Hopefully you will then be able to avoid appearing in the "News" pages of certain well known waterway publications.

"Dropping paddles" is of course something of a misnomer. They should never be allowed to crash down - risking the racks and rods shearing off the pin at the top of the paddle. A less obvious risk is that if allowed to drop all the way under their own weight they tend to bounce slightly and re-engage the ratchet leaving the paddle slightly open - a possible cause of a low pound.

"Dropping" means either winding down or allowing the ratchet bar or square end to rotate in your hand until a few inches short of a crash, at which point you grab tight so that the final impact is as gentle as winding. Although this latter technique plays havoc with delicate skin it saves a lot of winding, energy and time - with no detriment to the lock gear.

Remember also that speedy/efficient lock working should not entail rushing round - just quiet, unhurried, *unwasted* movements with the boat spending as greater proportion of the time as possible moving, either horizontally or vertically.

In **broad** locks the ideas are basically the same, except of course it's not so easy to nip across the roof etc. A centre or back end (rail) line is a wise precaution. A single round-turn (remember that?) on a "convenient" bollard, with the end trailed straight along the ground will usually give sufficient friction to stop the boat moving about and yet still prevent it from hanging up.

The main problem with broad locks and a single boat is that, as you enter from the top or leave the bottom, the other gate will tend to open. This is a simple but inevitable consequence of fluid dynamics. At the top I use a short shaft on the handrail to pull the opposite gate shut. Unfortunately this tends to pull the stern over as well (equal and opposite reactions and all that) so you will need to use the shaft again to push back over and shut the original top gate. On leaving the bottom, the bottom gates being heavier, simply going slowly out usually prevents movement but if you have a crew to shut your gate, or an oncoming boat, then a good burst of throttle as your counter goes through the gap tends to push more water into the chamber and ensure the offside gate stays shut.

One curious thing though is the way that, when any lock is almost empty, the boat tends to move away from the bottom gate back toward the cill. Apart from being indicative of the fact that the gates should now open, and keeping the boat out of the way, (perhaps hitting the top cill) I have never fully understood this. I used to think it was a reflected wave from a downstream lock or bridge but it happens on clear, straight pounds and rivers as well - so I am reduced to thinking of it as the result of the forward inertia of **all** the water leaving the lock. When there is no more water entering the pound (from the emptying lock) there may be a slight "hole" left behind which the water has to come back and refill.

I am not entirely happy with this explanation I must admit but it does also explain why a similar thing can happen when ones bows are at the head of the lock waiting for the lock to fill and just as you achieve "a level" the boat tends to move back from the gate albeit to a lesser extent than when the boat is in the lock. In this case the suggestion is that water is slightly heaped in the chamber - having been pushed there by the inertia of the movement of the upstream level.

Both these anomalies only seem to occur on locks that fill or empty rapidly - which tends to confirm these hypotheses. Atherstone locks fill very slowly - and no effect is observed. They empty very rapidly however and the bottom gates often then open several inches by themselves and water can be seen to re-enter the chamber.

Locks: Other Thoughts.

The pros and cons of leaving a boat in gear against the bottom gates of a narrow lock when descending have become something of a moot point. The particular worry here is that the bows may lodge on the top of the breast posts and failure to take immediate action could result in the boat sinking. It has been suggested that steel or steel composite gates are potentially more to blame here. Many wooden gates are so well mitred that you cannot let the bows go down the groove anyway but the alternative risk here is that the bows tend to go more sideways and may catch on uneven brickwork etc. in the lock wall. The only realistic answer is constant attention as mentioned in an earlier section. Do not chat casually to gongoozlers or fetch a pint from the pub unless you or a trusted crew member can actually *see* that the boat is going up or down evenly.

Some boaters use a tiller string (see below, page 42) in broad locks to keep the boat to the required side - both while waiting to enter an emptying lock and when in a filling lock. They use the "back end" line (that is the line attached to the rail or rings on the *front* of the engine room at the **back end** of the *hold*) to keep the boat parallel to the wall. With an empty unconverted boat this should behave perfectly. As stated previously though my preference is for a bow (or maybe mast?) line and to keep the boat *diagonal* in the lock. This makes it much harder for the bows to move about. With a fully converted or loaded boat this movement is much more likely - especially I might add again in the abnormally vicious broad locks on the Trent and Mersey Canal east of Burton on Trent.

As I have stated before, use whatever works for you. Remember however that there is more than one way of doing everything.

On the subject of filling broad locks incidentally, the order in which the paddles are raised can make quite a difference in ensuring a smooth passage.

The first paddle to be raised should be the ground paddle on the *same* side as the boat. The main force from this goes *under* your bows, bounces off the opposite wall and then holds your bows against the desired side. The second paddle should be the *opposite* gate paddle (if present) as the water from this (these) again tends to hold the bows in their designated place. Next is the opposite ground paddle followed, finally, by the gate paddle on the same side as the boat.

If you are sharing a broad lock with another narrow boat then the order of lifting paddles is probably irrelevant **provided that the bows are next to each other - NOT** the sterns. If sharing with a relatively fragile cruiser then raise the paddles in the order described above - again with the bows together. Many cruiser owners are rather timid of this - fearing that your bows will crush them. The real fear is that if your bows go sideways when their boat is half way along your length they will be subject to **twice as much crushing force** - this is a simple lever action. The further back they are, the worse it could be. Having said all this, although I have heard some horrible scrunching noises on occasions, I have *never* heard of a cruiser being crushed and sunk or even severely damaged in this way. Several boats (including narrow boats) have been sunk by getting "cross winded" or lodged diagonally through the inattention of their owners though.

Going downhill in broad locks, if the top gates are shut as you arrive, a common technique is to put the bows of the boat in the angle between gate and the gate recess on the side which you do **not** intend to open (ie generally the far or non-towpath side) and leave the boat diagonally with her stern against the other (ie nearer or towpath) side. She will usually remain in this position but you may have to leave her in gear with a tiller string (see below) set depending on the prevailing wind and other conditions. Adopt this position GENTLY and with care in regard to the position of ground paddle posts - which big ex-Grand Union boats are particularly prone to damaging.

When the lock is full, close the paddles on the side where the bows are, push them backwards if you can and return across the lock to open the unobstructed gate. Finally, go into reverse gear and give the stern a good push away from the bank. This should cause the boat to spin on her axis and bring the bows into line with the open gate for you to steer straight in. Don't use the engine to move away from the side as a blast of water straight from the counter is powerful enough to dislodge bricks and erode the bank (as witness many lock approaches 50 -70 feet from the lock entrances). There is also a tendency for the boat to sit down on a shallow bottom and you won't move at all. Neither should you go too fast or the other gate will swing open as well. This is because water pushed in front of your bows tries to leave the lock. If the other gate does start to open counteract this by pulling on its handrail, as described previously, as your boat's stern passes - either manually or with the short shaft.

On deep narrow locks with no ladder, leave the boat in gear again to enter the lock on her own but take a line off to enable you to stop or control her. If there is a bridge across the tail then take the short shaft instead and use it from the lockside to hook up the line from the cabin top as the boat enters. Don't forget to put the shaft back on the boat!

Some locks (eg Marple or on parts of the Staffs and Worcs) have provision for climbing the gates. Providing you treat them with the same caution you would treat any wet and slimy ladder, these are at least as safe as the more "cruiseway standard" version but people seem to have some strange illogical fears about them. Perhaps it's the lack of white paint or the idea that any object can only have one useful purpose. Most likely it's ignorance, the shortest answer to which is "Use it or Lose it".

Tiller and Rudder Strings

I will expand here on the use of tiller strings (or rudder strings as they have sometimes been called - but see below). I did mention them in "Uphill Problems" but perhaps further explanation is required.

The traditional version is to have two short lengths of cord, each with a loop in one end and the other end fixed to the cabin top, either side of the slide, just on the inside of the handrail (One is just visible in the photograph on page 55). The lengths are made such that either loop can be slipped over the end of the tiller to hold it to one side or the other. The idea being that when in forward gear the stern will always tend to move toward the desired side.

An alternative version has the two strings of such length that they can "both" be slipped over the end of the tiller and thus keep it straight. This version is more usually reserved for butties where it helps keep the butty straight when being towed and the steerer (if you have one) wants a break.

The "Chris Deuchar" version attaches the strings to the top corner of each door furthest from the hinges. With the doors closed you can use both strings to keep the tiller straight. With the doors open you can hold the tiller to either side. You therefore have the best of both worlds.

Tiller strings were also used with pairs of boats on the Grand Union and elsewhere when breasted up. There are several published photographs of horse boats with the tiller ends and rudder blades tied so that one steerer can manage both (typically empty) boats. One string goes from tiller "handle" to tiller handle and the other string from the hole in one rudder blade to the hole in the other. I have only seen one photograph of the same thing being used with a working motor/butty combination. This is perhaps partly due to the greater difficulty in readily passing a rope through the hole in the motor rudder blade and partly due to the greater amount of spare engine power available to overcome the inefficiencies of a lop-sided steering system compared with the horse drawn or manual version. Either way, those of you who go pair boating on broad canals or rivers might like to give it consideration.

I have always understood a *rudder* string to be a line attached to the hole in the rudder. These are typically seen on butty or horse boats used as above or to tie the 'elum to one side to reduce the likelihood of damage in locks. To summarise, a *tiller* string is to be attached to the *tiller* and a *rudder* string to a *rudder*. Okay?

Locks: Finalé.

During the original publication of this series it was suggested that we, the hNBOC, should also record horse boating techniques. Although this was outside my original intentions, viz. to present old established techniques for the benefit of the motor powered boater of *today*, I resolved to include as many horse boating items as I could. This was not only for the sake of completeness but also in case other readers might identify a potential use which I had missed.

The first technique of which I *am* aware was to use a small pulley block on the mast through which a rope was passed to a bollard or similar so that something approaching a two-to-one purchase enabled the horse to start in "low gear". The really clever bit however, was a small wooden toggle (similar to that on your IWA burgee - or any other flag) which was spliced in the line between bollard and mast at a distance such that after the boat had moved a certain amount the toggle reached the block and the horse changed from low gear to "top gear". The bollard end of the line would then go slack and you could lift the rope off the bollard easily. To refine this further a suitable slip knot could be used on the bollard (see Slippery Hitch in section 7 - Knots) so that it would just fall off as the boat left, to be coiled up on the move. Some canals (especially the, Worcs and Brum) had special "blocking hooks" for this purpose. These are a simple iron hook on its side, set near each top gate, so that a backwards pull, as when leaving the lock with the blocks set as described, kept the line in place, but a forwards pull, as the boat left, simply pulled the line off.

Today's bollards tend to be spaced far too erratically, and this is all probably too complex for the average single hander to use just to get out of the lock and shut the gate anyway, but feel free to experiment - carefully!

Another "knotty" problem is dealing with lock bridges - particularly at places like Foxton and other staircases where a narrow footbridge stops the single hander from pulling the boat in and out with a rope.

Going downhill is not too bad provided you have remembered to keep a suitable rope with you on the lockside as the boat descends. A suitable rope is of course

Using the blocking hook (just visible on right, below beam) on the W & B Canal

one which will allow you to get the boat as far out of the lock as possible before letting go. In a narrow lock this could be the stern line (not just looped over a dolly though, or it may well "ping off" - use a lark's head knot [see section 7] or similar) but in a broad lock a centre or "back end" line will give more control.

Going uphill means that you can pull the boat forward with a stern line. Once in the lock however you either have to climb down a ladder or hook up a rope with the short shaft and ...oh dear you forgot to bring it with you - Again!

Using a light line bent (eg sheet bend) to your bow, centre or "back end" line, you can throw a suitably heavily knotted end (try the "monkey's fist" found in most knot books, a multi-turned figure of eight knot - or tie on a small piece of wood) back towards the boat whilst holding onto the excess coils. Done correctly the knotted end will swing under the bridge and all but catch you on the back of the head! Grab this (the rope end of course - NOT your head) and then use the main rope to control the boat in the lock. Like most such techniques, it looks easy, but it took me a while to get the knack. It's another one of those things that are best practised without the boat and when no one is about. It is best to throw away and slightly *upward* if anything so that the rope's end is able to gather the maximum momentum on its downward path to swing back up the other side of the bridge.

Courtesy at locks

One aspect of lock working which seems to have declined enormously in a very few years is what I shall call **lock courtesy**. A surprising number of today's boaters tackle each lock as it comes and will work it totally independently from start to finish for themselves - from opening the first paddle to closing the last gate. Only on completion will they make any attempt to observe the rest of the world.

There will always be those first-timers who arrive at a lock in a flight, get off en masse, work the boat through the lock en masse, get back on board en masse and proceed to the next lock to start the whole thing again with never a thought for sending a crew member ahead to get things ready. In a spaced out flight it is an irritation but in the thick of Audlem (Yes! I have seen it) it is absurd. Suggesting lock wheeling to such a crew generally gets you such a look of sheer admiration that you almost forget to mumble that it is the way most people do it.

I'm starting to digress yet again so, in brief, try to remember the following:-

On arrival at a lock through which you intend to pass *immediately* (most definitely NOT after you have filled up from the water point, emptied the Elsan, had lunch etc etc in *any* order), DO NOT fill or empty the lock for yourselves unless you have first checked
a) that it safe to do so
b) there is no queue
c) there is no boat within reasonable sight which *might* be intending to pass through the lock if it is already in (or nearly in) their favour. If they intend to pass then open the gates for them. If they have set the lock and are sat beyond on the water point, emptying the Elsan, having lunch etc etc then ask if they are intending to pass through because, if they are not ready you "...will just nip through first...". Be polite and they will either suddenly realise the tanks are full, the Elsan was

empty all along and they had *just* finished the washing up OR they will say "Okay. Go ahead".

On entering the lock with any spare space, check that there is no other boat behind you which could share the work with you. There will always be the odd one who will join you for a free ride. If it's just for one or two locks then ignore their ignorance and give yourself a pat on the back for saving water. If they really refuse to do any work in a flight then you could try stopping in the middle one and saying it's their turn now - but you may decide it's not worth it. The exception to this is when the other boat is being worked single handed and you have a multiple crew. Obviously it would unfair to expect any more than token help in this case. (Happy boating single handers!)

Having, at last, got into the lock, closed the gates behind you and indulged in any necessary rope play, CHECK before you wind the paddles at the far end that no one beyond is struggling to manoeuvre otherwise you will probably make a bad situation worse and could well be delayed as an indirect result of your own haste if they get stuck across your path.

Similarly, when going down a flight of locks with short intermediate pounds which are all running weir, do not empty a full lock into a full pound without first winding up the paddles to fill the next lock down. Again, this is hard work for the single hander (use a bike?) but the difference in depth in the intermediate pound may be worsened by inches if you fill the next lock *after* the water from the lock you are in has all gone over the weir. More haste, less speed, again if you get stuck as a result - quite apart from the unnecessary wastage of water.

On leaving the lock, if it is appropriate to shut the gates, look along the canal first to check whether anyone wants to come in. Why make work for yourself - and them? ...but many people do! The same of course applies when you have just passed a movable bridge. Make sure however that the oncoming boat is not only intending to pass but also realises that the bridge should be kept shut. They may not have seen you open it.

Finally, if you are following another boat through a series of locks and you are repeatedly getting to the next lock before they leave, offer to close their last gate(s) for them. This "extra" work will actually speed you *both* up as they will be able to leave sooner, therefore get to the next lock sooner and there will be less likelihood of you waiting for them. Similarly, if another boat is following **you** then ask them to close the gates when you leave - to speed things up. If you are in the middle of a series of boats of course you are doing *exactly the same work* as if you were the only boat. The first boat is doing slightly less and the last boat is doing slightly more - *this* time. Its swings and roundabouts of course in the longer term.

Chapter 9. DEALING WITH RIVERS

I was lucky in that my boating interest started with rivers and then later encompassed canals. It was many years before I realised that people who started on canals tended to have a disproportionate fear of rivers - as did many former working boaters. Yes, there are extra dangers, it is far easier to drown in a river than a canal but, treated with the respect one should give to any work of nature, any extra danger should be negligible.

Any river, however small, still requires respect. If in any doubt about what you will find, insist on all crew wearing life jackets (or at least buoyancy aids) and have an anchor ready as well as spare ropes. These are simple, sensible, elementary precautions to take when dealing with even the shortest of river sections for at least the first time - whether it is the Trent at Alrewas or the Cherwell below the Rock of Gibraltar. Even the best swimmers may have a heart attack falling into cold water on a hot day. Unless they are wearing some sort of life jacket they will sink - and die because, in the deep, moving water of a river they can't be found in time to resuscitate them. This is a regrettably common occurrence.

On a canal (as when driving along a narrow road) you should be constantly thinking, "What would I do if something came the other way round the corner NOW?". On a river it is wise to also think… "What would I do if the engine stopped NOW?". The panic reaction is to drop the anchor but this could well turn out to be more of a liability than a help. If you do drop anchor what will you do next? What will the boat do next? Will you have to wade or swim ashore? Will the boat swing round in the current or wind and jam across the waterway?

Engines rarely stop instantaneously. Even if they do, the boat will probably have enough residual momentum to reach the nearest bank if you have thought about it in advance as I have suggested. When you reach the bank take care in getting a rope ashore. Beware of underwater rocks stopping the boat abruptly and jettisoning you in the water. Beware of crumbling banks and get a round turn from the rope around *something* (probably not an angler though) as quickly as possible before you stop and take stock of your situation.

As for actual navigation on rivers, a few obvious basics. Firstly, you will go faster down stream than up. In flood conditions you will be able to go much faster downstream but it may not be possible to go upstream at all. Another less obvious result of any amount of rain is that not only will the river be deeper but the headroom under bridges will be less. This latter is potentially the most dangerous. All in all, if you don't know a river, it is much safer to go *up* the first time. You can stop more quickly. You can stop completely (see "traversing" below). And you don't have to worry so much about unexpected weirs. There are problems nevertheless with certain waterway rings where you must go down one river to go up another. My personal suggestions are that you should go down the Severn and up the Avon (Warwickshire *or* Bristol!), down the Aire and up the Trent, down the Trent and up the Soar, up the Thames and down the Grand Union (whether for the London ring or the Oxford ring). Looking to the future, you should go down the Manchester Ship Canal and up the Weaver.

As many of you will know, the current in a river does not always take the shortest path. In a typically meandering river, the fastest current will swing to the *outside* of all bends and will change from one side to the other a little downstream of the mid point between adjacent bends. Proceeding upstream then, you will get along better if you tend to cut corners to reach what is called the "slack water". In narrow rivers, such as the Soar or Nene, this is not usually practical or worthwhile but on the major rivers it can save a lot of time and diesel. It is imperative however that you keep a good lookout for craft coming the other way, or those about to overtake you from behind. Other useful slack water can be found at the confluence of two rivers. Eddying water or floating leaves etc usually give this away. A particularly good example is where the waters from the Trent meet the waters from the Derbyshire Derwent head on at the eastern entrance to the Trent & Mersey Canal. Depending on the relative flows of the two rivers, the position of the slack water can vary by as much as 100 feet. Entering or leaving the canal by the slack water makes life much easier with a pair of boats - especially when the water is up.

Rights and Rules

This is probably a good point at which to mention a few points about rights of way. Firstly, unlike canals which are technically static water, a boat heading downstream has general right of way over one heading upstream - except of course where traffic lights or other specific local conditions dictate otherwise. This means that if you are heading upstream and approaching a bridge you must be prepared to give way to (ie. keep out of the way of) anything coming downstream. Like most maritime rules the reasoning is quite simply that it is easier for you, rather than the other boat, to do so.

Similarly, when overtaking another boat, it is your job to keep clear. The other boat should maintain its course and speed, but is under no other obligation to help you get by. Accordingly the onus is on you to make sure you have the time and space available. I mention this again (I referred to it earlier in the section on overtaking) because a hazard peculiar to rivers is that of sailing dinghies. These tend to use the maximum water space available when racing as the accumulation of each inch gained can save a tack and make the difference between winning and losing. I know, I used to sail.

For a couple of centuries there was another general rule that power should give way to sail. This was logical until the advent of the supertanker which simply *couldn't* readily give way to sail and so the rule was modified to read that power should give way to sail except when sail is overtaking *or where the powered boat, by virtue of its size or lack of manoeuvrability (including draught), is unable to do so.* To me a full length narrow boat has negligible manoeuvrability compared with a sailing dinghy and so should maintain a steady (and therefore *predictable* course) through the melée. In my sailing days it was much preferred when powered boats took this strategy rather than trying to weave through us. At the other extreme there were those who were so filled with contempt that they would happily speed through and see if they could knock us out of the way. Like most things it's all a question of balance and consideration for one's fellow man.

Remember, as I have mentioned previously, *your* boat may be the smaller vessel and *you* will be expected to get out of the way of significantly larger vessels whom it would be unreasonable to expect to take measures to avoid you. (See Gloucester and Sharpness Canal photograph on page 9)

Occasionally you may see a small, stationary boat carrying a blue flag. This indicates the presence of divers. You should slow down as much as possible, keep well clear and watch out for any signals.

"Blue Flagging" on the other hand is a continental technique used by skippers of moving vessels intending to pass on the "wrong" side. In other words instead of keeping to the right or "passing port to port" they wish to pass to the left. This is quite useful on bends where, as described before, vessels proceeding upstream will want to keep left on left hand bends to keep out of the current and oncoming vessels will also want to keep left on the same bend to keep *in* the current. Blue lights are used at night and the system seems better than the sometimes ambiguous or inaudible sound signal (two short blasts) given on British waterways. Our authorities have resisted proposals to change for reasons of which I am unaware. There is nothing stopping us adopting the technique *unofficially* though in the same way that lorry and other professional drivers flash their headlights. Break out the blue flags!

Sound signals

Finally, for this section, I will briefly mention the other common sound signals. These are much published elsewhere and so don't really fall within my mandate but I include them because knowledge of them is so poor on the canals and yet, when confronted by a commercial coaster on the Weaver or wherever, you will need to know what they mean!

> **One short** - I am altering course to starboard. (Rarely used as this is the default system)
> **Two short** - I am altering course to port (= Blue flagging)
> **Three short** - I am going astern
> (NB this does NOT necessarily mean you are going backwards!)
> **Four short followed after pause by one short** - I am about to manoeuvre to starboard
> **Four short followed after pause by two short** - I am about to manoeuvre to port
> **One long at 20 second intervals** - when approaching a bend, junction (lock?) etc

The above were taken from a British Waterways leisure document published in 1987.

A short blast is about one second and a long blast about five. I also seem to remember another signal that was pressed upon me this was "I am unable to manoeuvre". Unfortunately, the nature of this signal has been varied by different authorities to the extent that it has become ambiguous - at least to those who may only meet it once in their whole lives. The following signals should be sufficient - if not for complete understanding

- at least to make your "opponent" at least look to see what is going on:

Four short - I am unable to manoeuvre.
Five short - You are not taking sufficient action to avoid me!

Stopping - going *upstream*. (Nb. To allow for tidal situations, "upstream" means "against the flow" and vice versa throughout)

This is easy - unless you have a particularly perverse wind of course. As described in the section on mooring up the idea is to get the bows in first and a line safely ashore. The current will then do the rest and bring the stern in with maybe just a bit of help from you with the engine in forward gear and the tiller hard over in the direction you want the stern to go.

Of course you may not want to moor up, you may be waiting for a lock for instance, in which case try to match your forward speed to that of the river's flow. This will rarely be much above tick-over and with only slight movements of the tiller you should be able to remain stationary or "maintain station" as the yachting manuals call it.

Traversing

This is actually a canoeing term which I have appropriated for use here. Following on from "maintaining station" above, slight movements of the tiller will enable you to move from side to side across the river without actually moving forwards or back. This is an excellent technique to master for getting into busy riverside moorings (Evesham?, Thames? etc) where there might only be *just* enough space in between the gleaming white plastic for your freshly tarred hull. The speed of the sideways motion is largely dictated by the amount by which you move the tiller, provided these movements are kept small (otherwise the speed of the current and engine speed play a part in a "triangle of velocities").

Canoeists typically use traversing by back paddling when boating *downstream* to move sideways to go down a weir or other white water at the best point. I don't recommend this for narrow boat pairs!

Stopping - going *downstream*.

The recommended approach to be found in all the books (if you can find one) is that you should go past the point where you want to stop, turn round and then proceed upstream to moor as above. This is often impossible with a narrow boat of almost any length on rivers such as the Soar, Nene, Weaver, Severn at Gloucester etc..

The latter can be particularly dangerous if the lock is not ready for you to enter. Adopting the "bows on" approach in such circumstances may result in your stern swinging across the river and the boat becoming swept round in a strong current. What we have to do, is be prepared well in advance with a stern line, (incidentally don't just loop an eye over, use a lark's head knot or similar) and approach the bank, at low speed, on a near parallel course. When about a yard (~metre) away push the tiller hard toward the bank and reverse fairly hard. What should happen is that the bows will start to swing away, the stern will nudge the bank and you will engage neutral and step ashore to make fast the stern strap. The bows will then be brought back by the current. If not, engaging forward gear should help with a few "revs" on.

Always, for your *own* safety, engage neutral before stepping ashore with the rope.

Needless to say, its not always that easy, there often isn't a bollard for instance. Use a tree, a strong fence post (near the *base* remember to minimise leverage, not the top) or a hook. The latter is an "S" shaped piece of metal about ¾" (20mm) in diameter which can be used to clip on railings or ladders and gives you a convenient, instant place to loop your rope. Alternatively have a "δ" shaped hook with a rope permanently attached (anchor hitch?) which can then be hooked onto such a railing or rung in passing and then the other end *strapped onto a dolly*. Nb. do **not** tie directly or the resulting "twang" could pull away the iron work. As before, beware of using waterway "furniture" (in the architectural *or* literal sense of the word!) for purposes other than which they were originally designed. Mind you, the oil tankers and other carriers always used this technique and a single rope to steady themselves in the Trent locks - but perhaps they had specially strengthened ladders?

Another risk of course is in getting the stern strap caught in the "blades". Keep ropes tidy and ready for use at all times. Hanking (see drawings) is a very quick and simple technique for not only keeping ropes available for immediate use but also makes it easy to hang them up in the engine room (to dry?) when not boating. Hold the coil in one hand and choose any loop, other than the first or last, pull it sideways with the other hand and pass it *completely* around the hank and then *through* the hank to form a hanging loop.

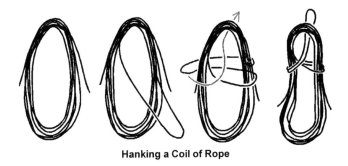

Hanking a Coil of Rope

Specific river problems.

There are lots of sections of river navigation where everyday navigation technique will get you through but where a bit of extra local knowledge will help. I mentioned the downstream approach to Gloucester Docks above and I mention a few more special places below.

(Nb. "upstream" and "downstream" revert to their normal usage from hereon)

Upstream to Cranfleet Lock, River Trent

After passing the site of Thrumpton Ferry (about ¾ mile downstream of the lock) and after passing the marked mud bank on the south bank (Nb. This is the rivers *right* bank as conventionally described - viewed from the rivers source - but it will of course be on your *left*) move over to the "wrong" side (ie your left, the river's right). Keep very close to the trees as the water is deep but slow flowing here compared with the "normal" navigation route. Keep an eye out for downstream craft and give two short blasts on the horn to indicate your wish to pass the "wrong" way. Keep on this side until you are almost alongside the lock on the other side of the river before traversing across.

Marton Rack, tidal Trent

This bend, near the village of Marton has the channel on the "wrong" side - in other words on the *inside* of the bend. There are other places (and sunken islands) on the tidal Trent where this occurs but none quite so severe or so badly signed (but this may have changed).

Downstream to enter West Stockwith Lock, River Trent/Chesterfield Canal

If you have given a good estimate of arrival time, or used "Narrow Boats On Cellnet", then the lock will hopefully be ready for you to enter carefully. Otherwise you will have to tie up and wait at the piling just upstream of the lock entrance.

When the tide is running out (ie "ebbing" - the usual situation) then adjacent to this piling the current flows *upstream* in a strange eddy. This means you can approach from upstream and stop with ease without turning.

If you are coming down against the tide (unusual if you have obeyed the lock keepers directions elsewhere) then the eddy tends to disappear - ie the direction of tide and eddy are the same - and you can stop in identical fashion to the foregoing.

Downstream to enter Trent Lock, River Trent/Erewash Canal

As the Erewash entrance is at an acute angle to the river and facing downstream, the commonest way for boats to enter is to pass the entrance (making sure that the way is clear) turn round in the main body of the river and approach easily from downstream. To refine this slightly, there is a very large eddy in the Cranfleet Canal entrance whose speed of rotation depends directly on the rate of the river's flow. This turns anticlockwise and, if you do the same, it will help you round without going to close to the sailing club or Thrumpton Weir.

The "flashy" way to do it is to turn round (more than 90°) in the middle of the river *before you reach the entrance* and then just go ahead at the appropriate moment as you pass sideways in the river's current - again after ensuring that the way is clear. Just upstream of the lock and at the downstream end of the garden and landing stage for the Trent Navigation Inn, there is a triangular section of masonry which disguises a stream outfall. This is where you should start turning (slow down forward motion and then use plenty of revs to make a tight turn. Remember?) There is a small area of slack water under all navigable conditions above, and in front of, the entrance bridge. Just be aware that your bows will cease to go sideways when they hit it but the rest of the boat won't.

Other sites

The downstream approach to Selby lock on the Yorkshire Ouse can be "interesting". (A friend once pointed to exactly on my bow where I might expect to hit the stonework on the lock approach!) The entry to the River Wey from the Thames also has its foibles but in all these cases be particularly aware of how much the boat is being carried *sideways* and react accordingly. Far too much notice seems to be taken of which way the boat is pointing rather than the, much more important but subtle, way she is *going*.

An apology:- Re-reading through all the above, I feel I might sometimes have overstated things. Thousands (probably) of boats go safely through these manoeuvres regularly without an inkling of what I have been writing about. All I am trying to do here is give little pointers to help you do things better as I believe we should **all** be continually striving to improve our boating performance.

At the start of this work I emphasised that it was just a personal view. Furthermore I have regularly tried to point out potential dangers but feel I must remind you, (for my own legal protection!) that my comments are not intended to be taken as "gospel" and that they are given without any kind of guarantee other than that they have, except where stated, worked for me.

Chapter 10. WORKING WITH A BUTTY.

As I have stated before in these pages, it is necessary to constantly ask yourself, "What would I do if another boat came round the corner NOW?" If it does then the next question should be "Has it got a butty?"! - No, I know there aren't many of them about these days but if those of us who do occasionally "drag a trailer" tell the others how we do it then the opportunities for accidents and misunderstandings will hopefully be minimal. Like everything else in this guide, unless stated otherwise, these are just my own opinions which I offer to you in the absence of anything better.

I tend to think of different boating techniques in terms of the percentage concentration span needed to perform them. In other words, if you are in an outboard powered rubber dinghy you probably only need to concentrate on steering the boat for some 10% of the time to keep moving along and can watch the wildlife, talk to your companions or open another can of XXXX the rest of the time. A small cruiser probably requires 30% concentration, a 50ft modern narrow boat 50% and a deep draughted, full length historic narrow boat about 70%. On this scale, towing a butty on cross straps (see below) takes about 90% concentration. You can get away with less but your boating will suffer.

There are basically two ways of towing a butty. The first way involves using two very short ropes (ie the straps) so that the butty bows are within an inch of, or even in contact with, the motor boats stern fender. The second method involves the use of a single long line of a variety of possible lengths from (say) 25 feet to 100 feet or more. The first method has the great advantage that a butty steerer is virtually redundant as starting, stopping and, with care, steering are under the motor steerer's almost immediate control. The second method enables greater speeds to be achieved and has other advantages in special situations but needs a relatively skilled butty steerer and stopping involves, either slowing down very gradually, or running into something!

Cross straps

The butty bows will have two short ropes, of equal length and with an eye splice at either end, permanently attached to the "T" stud. When in motion, one strap will go either side of the stem bar. They will then cross over beneath the nose of the bows before having their free eyes slipped over a dolly on each side of the motor boat counter. Viewed from above they will make a $\propto$ shape. When using cross straps, the straps should be short enough so that the butty stem bar actually rests on the motor tip-cat fender. If this then causes fouling with the swan's neck then your fenders aren't big enough or are badly adjusted. One of the beauties of cross straps is that the motor steerer has enormous control over the butty's movements. At no time is this more important than when stopping. Correctly adjusted straps will mean that the butty just digs into the fender. On the other hand, if she is too loose, then the butty will shear off to one side or the other and a strap is likely to ping over the stem bar and you can have 10+ tons of boat hurtling sideways. This is only until the remaining slack is taken up, admittedly - but it could be dangerous or damaging so be aware of the risk. The same thing can also happen on tight turns.

I am sure most of you know this already, and could easily tie a couple of boats together in this way for a standing start, so I won't bother with further diagrams. What I suspect some of you don't know however, is how to do this on the move such as when leaving a broad lock or bankside mooring.

The technique is to start the motor boat forwards at a slow but steady speed. As the motor counter approaches the butty bows, take the engine out of gear and reach across for the nearest cross strap, pull the bows firmly sideways and slip the eye over the *nearest* dolly. Turn round and put the engine back in gear (at a fast tick over). While doing this be prepared for a gentle jolt as the strap tightens and the butty bows swing right across the stern. Pick up the second strap and slip it onto the spare dolly. The whole operation from picking up the first strap takes less than ten seconds. Crucial to success is the speed of the motor relative to the butty when the first strap tightens. Too fast and the jolt will be severe (the strap might even break), too slow and the bows will not swing across sufficiently. In the first case you may have to buy some new crockery and/or rope. In the second, if there is sufficient room to manoeuvre, slow down and push the tiller over to give a bit of extra overlap otherwise you will have to slow right down to sort it out.

There are other things to pay attention to. Firstly, there are numerous opportunities for fingers to get caught inside loops of rope. Keep them and all valued appendages well clear of both ropes and narrow gaps between boats. Secondly, mind you don't get jolted off the counter (this is only one reason for taking the engine out of gear when picking up the first strap). Practise carefully. The operation is also simplified if, prior to moving off, the nearest strap is laid backwards toward the cratch, just behind the cant, and the furthest strap is left to dangle as far forward as possible whilst remaining on the far side of the stem bar.

NOT how to rig cross straps! Note how the motor's wash is rebounding from the butty bows, the "snatcher" coiled on the counter, the lifted stern fender and the freshly spliced (broken?) strap. The shortening as a result of this probably causing the other problems.

Once moving along, there seems little difference initially compared with steering a single boat. However, if the butty tiller is left unattended, her stern will tend to swing to one side or the other and "stick". This is due to the hydrodynamics I discussed in one of the first chapters. As the stern gets closer to the bank, the current increases on the bank side, pressure drops and the boat moves even closer in. There are three ways to correct this. Firstly, let the butty steerer deal with it by steering firmly sideways. Secondly, in the absence of a butty steerer, use tiller strings to keep the butty steering straight ahead at all times. Thirdly prevent it from happening at all by careful steering *of the motor*. In case you haven't already noticed, as you move the tiller to keep the motor boat going in the proper direction, the butty stern will swing the *opposite* way. By taking care to keep the motor in the centre of the channel and making timely allowance for approaching bends and other craft it is not too difficult to keep the butty in the channel too and thereby progress more efficiently. Incidentally, with no butty steerer, it is often safest to deliberately "stick" the butty stern to the bank when passing oncoming craft and then give a good waggle with the motor to unstick her again.

I have so far assumed that your butty is a traditional unpowered boat. The term "butty" is generally agreed to be an old, English term meaning "mate". It is still used extensively in this form in the north of England and with its derivative "buddy" in America. (The other "butty", meaning sandwich is believed to be completely unrelated and connected with the use of butter!) *Any* towed vessel can therefore be a butty but towing a second motor boat is generally more difficult due to the poor flow of water to the rudder caused by the unused propeller.

In spite of the loss of efficiency caused by the flow of water from the motor's stern hitting the butty bows, this is partly counteracted by the fact that the butty bows tend to slightly support the motor counter and stop it digging in so deep.

It is also worth noting that the butty steerer can influence the motor. The motor's bows will tend to go in the same direction as the butty tiller (and stern) is pushed. Thus, over-enthusiastic butty steerers can severely mess things up on tight corners. The butty steerer should try and keep the butty in line with the motor boat under normal circumstances - but I have dealt with this more thoroughly in the later section on butty steering.

Long lines

On cross straps, the butty bows can absorb a lot of energy from the motor's wake and slow you down. This is increasingly true the deeper the butty is in the water. With a loaded butty you'll barely move at all, so the main attraction of using a long line is that you can get along faster. On the debit side the butty needs steering all the time and the steerer needs to remember that they have no brakes. If the motor stops unexpectedly, the motor steerer could theoretically use the butty line and strap both boats to a halt with engine assistance but, in practice, they are more likely to be taking avoiding action themselves or trying to keep the towing line out of the "blades". The only realistic option for stopping the butty is therefore to run into something. Many historic motors have dented counters which testify to one option, the alternative option is to graze to a halt along the bank. Although it is not uncommon for the ends of elm bottoms to be protected by metal "shoeing" strips nailed along the whole length of the boat either side, sometimes this is only done on the forward quarters as this is where most wear occurs.

In the normal way of things, whilst on the move, the butty steerer should aim to keep the butty bows about in line with one side or the other of the motor's hull. This keeps the butty out of the propeller's wake whilst still keeping the towing line as straight as possible.

Long lines come in two general forms. The first is typically some twenty feet in length and is called a *snatcher* and goes from a dolly on the motor counter to the butty T stud (as in the photograph on page 59). This is great for going quickly round a series of relatively sharp corners or between locks where breasting up is impractical. It is easily handled and doesn't get in the way too much. The second form is at least seventy feet long (in times past it could be nearly 200 feet) and is called a *snubber*. This usually went from the motor dolly, or hook if there was one, to the butty mast. Such practice is best left for loaded boats so that the mast can be extended to allow the snubber to clear the butty cratch. Raising the mast on an unladen boat, whilst practical, "just isn't done"!

Running Blocks

A variant on the snubber was to use running blocks. Last seen in regular use on the Nurser built butty *Lucy* when working for the now defunct Blue Line, these left the control of the line length, literally, in the hands of the butty steerer. The technique has been well described elsewhere but I will describe it briefly here to complete the subject. Instead of being terminated at the butty mast, the line passed through a pulley block attached to the mast and then through holes in three wooden blocks, fitted with rollers, which were lashed to the top planks. The line was then fixed to a removable T stud fixed by the cabin slide, within reach of the steerer. Not only could line length be controlled to the optimum but the butty steerer could keep slack line away from the motor's blades. Another major advantage was that the motor steerer could set off faster when leaving locks etc and the butty steerer could strap the butty into motion using the T stud rather than receiving a jolt. On the debit side, the coils of rope in the butty hatches could be both dirty at best and hazardous at worst when strapping.

On the subject of fast getaways, one can use the horse boat "low gear" technique, described in chapter 8: Locks - finalé, for leaving double or paired locks but substituting the motor boat for the horse. To me, the highlight of a trip along the North Oxford Canal with a butty, is the passage of Hillmorton Locks where you can carry the butty's mast line to the motor and both boats can be leaving almost together - none of the messing about associated with resetting cross straps. As I said in the chapter on single locking, the aim should be that both boats should be moving horizontally *or* vertically as much as possible and be completely stationary for the minimum time.

Butties and locks

Taking a breasted up pair through a double lock is inevitably virtually identical to taking a single boat through a single lock and I won't dwell on it further. Taking a pair along the canal at all is also something of a minority sport, but even those without traditional butties may occasionally tow someone else's boat if, say, broken down and hopefully the following may help. I shall assume initially that cross straps are being used.

On reaching an unready lock take the motor bows to the bank as described before and leave the rest to float at will. Generally the boats will jack-knife (enabling the butty steerer disembark to set the lock) but this doesn't really matter. As described before, it is important to keep the motor stern in deep water. Obviously if there are other boats nearby, more care will have to be taken. It is also courteous to warn any anglers that they may have to move their nets. Only if they object will you need to remind them (and any moored boat(s)) that they should leave 150 feet of bank free. Not only do the byelaws support you but also the code of conduct for anglers.

Whoever sets the lock can firstly tie the motor bow rope to a convenient bollard/ tree/ fence etc (younger anglers might even enjoy holding the rope for you!) and then open one gate, untie and push the bows back into the channel. This should straighten out the whole "rig" enough for the motor to be steered into the lock. On a single lock you will have to "loose off" the butty in the tail of the lock, just outside the gates. Don't bother to tie her up at this stage (unless you have a spare crew member with nothing better to do), just throw her bow rope or masthead towing line onto the bank as a precaution. This should be thrown on the *upstream* side of any lock bridge of course. The butty will normally sit patiently, at least long enough for you to close the gates and start the lock filling or emptying, before requiring further attention - if any. Whilst the motor is locking through, you can save time by laying the butty bow or tow rope between the tops of the breast posts on the gates. Thus, when the lock is re-emptied for the butty, you can pull the boat in and open both bottom gates simultaneously.

On a double lock the motor enters through one gate. When it is about half way in, let go the strap attached to the dolly **furthest** from the wall *before slowing down*. The butty will then swing hard against the wall and you can push the tiller away from the wall and engage reverse gear hard before letting go the other strap. Ideally the butty will continue, under her own momentum, to force her way into the vee thus created and push the whole length of the motor against the wall behind the gate you *didn't* open. This will simulta-neously slow the butty down so that she may require a little manual help before you can tie the sterns together using either a breast rope or, preferably, a diagonal rope from the motor's anser pin to the butty hook or T stud.[1]

If both gates are already open, the technique is similar but the motor goes in the same side that you intend her to end up and the butty gets a better chance to move over on the one strap. This means she could be going much faster so the whole approach can be slicker or

---

[1] Most regular "pair boaters" keep a short strap, with an eye spliced at either end, permanently attached to a shackle on each of the motor anser pins. These are of such a length that the butty will lie exactly alongside when they are tight. When not in use they are laid on the back deck, just inside the cants, or across the back of the cabin. Another, longer, rope is used on each of the butty anser pins. This only has a loop at the end attached to the shackle and the free end can then be used as a brake for the butty by strapping onto one of the motor dollies, or a bollard, as appropriate.

slower depending upon your confidence level at the time! There is so much that can go wrong with a butty that I am only going to mention the worst pitfalls as they crop up. A common error is for the motor to slow down before the butty has moved over. She will invariably go the *wrong* side and jam on the strap. You then either have to stop and push the butty back or *speed up* to swing her back - if the space is available. Fingers are especially at risk but, generally though, keep all bits of your body out of gaps between boats, gaps between boats and walls and gaps between moving ropes and anything else. Boats and contents are much more easily replaced than people are. If this isn't enough encouragement for care, remember that a recommended procedure for getting a patient, and their severed finger, to hospital is for them to put it in *their* mouth.

Leaving the Lock

Leaving the lock is very similar to the usual starting off procedure described earlier in this chapter. In fact this technique will allow you to get both boats out through the motor's gate. One point that is often missed is that with a single lock (and only slightly less true with a double lock) the butty will come out straight. Yes, so what? Yes, ...so that if you have fixed both cross straps then the motor stern will come out on the same straight line as the whole of the butty. Yes, ...so that if *both* boats aren't completely on a straight line they will jack-knife once again and surprise the boat that is waiting to go in the opposite direction through the lock. In other words, if you can't come straight out, then only fix *one* cross strap to give yourself some room to manoeuvre and fix the second when you are clear.

In flights of closely spaced locks it is usual to keep the boats separate and haul the butty manually. You may find the "low gear" technique most useful when working downhill but use the gate as a lever in conjunction with a slippery hitch (see Part 7.) working uphill. It largely depends on the availability and agility of your crew. For bowhauling between locks use the longest line possible from the mast. Seventy feet is really too short, 150 feet is a much better proposition. Shorter lines can be used but the boat tends to come towards the bank. This can be counteracted to some extent by tying the towing line to a point further aft - if you can find one - there is how-

Leaving Tyrley top lock with the snatcher set.

ever an increased sideways pull and so longer lines are to be preferred.

I have not actually described the process of breasting up when on the move. This is much the easiest in a bridge hole or lock entrance. Unfortunately these are not always available and, for mooring against the bank, I use a similar technique to that described for entering a double lock, thus tying both boats together before tying either to the bank. I have a single breast rope permanently attached to the butty bows which has an eye splice which will just reach to go over the motor T stud. (This rope is also extremely useful in other situations for temporary butty moorings at locks and the like.) At the stern the two lines from the anser pins cross diagonally and are tied tight onto the opposite boat. In combination these avoid the to-ing and fro-ing which lead to poor manoeuvring and unnecessary lurching about. By far the most difficult manoeuvre however is to breast up in mid channel. Although rarely necessary, this requires good coordination between steerers and good balance on the part of the one (usually the motor steerer) who has to run along and tie the fore ends together. There seems to be no way round this.

The only other thing worth mentioning in this section is what to do with the motor when working the butty through a single lock. Going uphill its easy, leave it in the head of the lock, in neutral, against the gate. Alternatively use a short line from the butty bows to the motor dolly and leave her in forward gear so that the butty starts to move as soon as you open the gate. Don't miss the boat! Going downhill the motor can wait in the tail. Use reverse in tick over though and remove the tiller, and tiller pin, as the rudder tends to thrash about in the turbulence as the lock empties and could break the tiller or knock even the wary overboard. Only *very* rarely is this turbulence sufficient to flush the motor away and even then she will come back to you if left in reverse as suggested. A far greater risk is that leaks from the bottom gates will swamp the counter so shut the doors *and* slide. Also, **always** remove the butty tiller in locks as they are much more prone to damage themselves as well as being capable of possibly splitting a traditional butty ram's head. In fact, except when moored at the end of the days boating, with the tiller pointing upwards of course, the butty tiller should always be removed and laid on the cabin top when not actually being used for steering. This way it will not be forgotten sometime.

Steering a butty

This is a rather different technique from steering a motor boat. In fact there are two distinct techniques.

On a long line, whether loaded or unloaded, the biggest difference is that everything seems to happen so much slower. Without the power from a propeller to push a rapidly flowing stream of water onto the rudder blade, you are solely reliant on the flow of water as you move through it. This is much slower and therefore much less effective. In fact, if you are not moving at all relative to the water (even if you are drifting down a river) you will have absolutely no steerage - a point my school geography teacher was completely unable to grasp I might add. He was firmly of the opinion that Rhine barges could drift down the river in full control of their destination. You might like to try it sometime!

The only way you *can* use the rudder in such a situation is to give vigorous thrusts on the tiller to *create* a flow and present day butty steerers frequently do this to assist their towers on tighter turns. An alternative was to drift downstream *backwards*, trailing a mud weight from the bows. The drag from this then provided the flow past the rudder required for its use and enabled the craft to move from one side to the other. This technique was commonly used to get unpowered boats to their destinations on millstreams and river backwaters where there was either no towpath or no turning place.

Apart from this slowness for anything to happen, and the complete lack of brakes, a butty on a long line is not *so* different from a motor boat.

On cross straps however things are *completely* different. The essential thing for the butty steerer to remember is to push the tiller in the direction they want the *stern* to go and to only do this *when necessary*.

This simple statement inevitably disguises a whole number of subtleties. It is also often in contradiction to what would be expected from a motor boat steerer. To make a motor boat move to the right, you push the tiller to the left, with the butty you *will* push the tiller to the right. With frequent changes from cross straps to "no straps", on entering broad locks alongside the motor boat, the butty steerer will have to rapidly switch between these conventions. To do this well requires quite a competent steerer, familiar with both techniques, and is not the easy job it may appear. At the other end of the scale though, I mentioned above that the steerer should only steer when necessary. This is the "cop out" for the inexperienced because it really is easier if the butty steerer does absolutely nothing rather than be over enthusiastic and get it wrong.

Let us start with a "training" scenario then and see how it might progress. Having cast off with our trainee on the butty, we have told them to keep the tiller in the middle unless told otherwise. Along the initial straight all is well, the motor steerer inherently corrects minor variations in the butty's path. On going round the first bend however there is a tree on the outside.... and the butty is swinging crabwise into it.... tell the butty steerer to push the tiller to the *inside* of the bend.... "Isn't that the wrong way?", "NO, do it!". It's done and a scrape on the paintwork is avoided. Back to the straight.

Next a bridge, with a bend beyond. After steering the motor through and starting the turn, the butty is cutting the corner.... the cabin will hit the underside of the brick arch.... tell the butty steerer to hold the tiller to the *outside* of the bend.... "That's not what you told me before?", "FOR GOODNESS SAKE DO IT! And mind the tiller doesn't catch on the brickwork!....". And so on. Gradually the butty steerer learns to ignore the front of his boat - it is after all tied directly to the motor stern, whose steerer will guide it in the right place.

So butty steerers, watch for sideways crabbing, and keep the middle and stern away from *everything*.

The next phase is where the butty steerer has got the hang of all this contra-steering and starts to anticipate events. This can be dangerous and a bad butty steerer can make life very hard for the motor steerer - so it pays not to fall out with each other!

As I said above, pushing the butty tiller to the right will move the stern part of the boat to the right. The motor boat stern is relatively immovable but will still *tend* to be pushed to the left by this. This in turn moves the motor's bows to the right - the whole combination tends toward a slight "jack-knife" arrangement. If you don't believe me, get your butty steerer to try a brief, but abrupt, movement of their tiller to one side and back when on a straight length and watch it happen. This is not normally a problem, but on bends, if the butty steerer pre-empts the turn, it makes it that much harder to get round as the motor rudder has to go further over, which slows everything down that bit more and so on. Remember the butty is some 70 feet behind the motor, they shouldn't therefore start the turn until 70 feet later. Waiting this time will then enable the butty bows to push the motor stern toward the outside of the bend, hence bringing its bows to the inside and potentially tightening the turn. In practice this means the motor rudder is moved *less* thereby reducing the drag from it and keeping the overall speed up.

Other butty steering details, around locks and so on, have been dealt with in their place and so I refer you elsewhere to these.

Chapter 11. LOADED BOATS

There is a well known quote from Kenneth Grahame's classic "Wind in the willows" which says something along the lines that there is "Nothing, absolutely nothing quite so much fun as messing about in boats". If this is true then there is absolutely no aspect of boating which is better than messing about with *loaded* boats. It is like no boating you have ever done before.

At the start of the original series (which I never expected to last as many years as it did) I set out to give a few thoughts of my own to those who were new to boating with craft which come close to the maximum passable dimensions on the narrow canals and to share ideas with the more experienced. As well as passing on some traditional methods in their own right, the idea was to put them in a modern context and add some newer ideas appropriate to the present day pleasure (but deep draughted) boater. I felt however that I could not let the series conclude without a brief chapter on both loading and carrying.

British Waterways currently require a commercial licence for all boats engaged in the carriage of freight. This is a wide definition which includes a boat's use as a workshop, as a tug and, depending on your waterway manager, a shop. As far as most people are concerned, freight means heavy bulk carriage such as coal, gravel or timber. Such carriage has made a small, but significant, comeback in the last few years due, at least in part, to the efforts of the Commercial Narrow boat Operators Association. After a number of years of carrying being left to those "who took a couple of tons of coal for a ride" in their summer holidays, there are now a dedicated few who do such work full time - as well as an increasing number of part-timers.

I could continue on this (largely irrelevant) discourse indefinitely so I will cut it short by suggesting Tim Wilkinson's "Hold on a Minute" as compulsory, and inspiring, reading!

Loading

Cargoes such as timber and palleted goods, either have to be loaded laboriously by hand, or by machine when appropriate. Conveyors don't present too much of a problem as the loading can be done gently and with minimal effort and the boat moved back or forward to give a level load. Considerable care is needed however when loading loose goods such as coal or gravel from a lorry. The greatest care is needed on the part of the lorry driver but, unfortunately, he will probably never have loaded a boat before, so you will have to educate him (and yourself) simultaneously.

Opinions differ on whether you should load starting from the front or back end of the hold. When you know a particular wharf, cargo and lorry driver well enough, it won't matter, but until then why not start in the middle? This way if you get it wrong you won't have so much shovelling to do! The main problem with starting at the back end is that the stern will dip and may touch bottom and prevent you moving the boat until the load is levelled. Frequently the lorry hardstanding is restricted and so it will not be possible to move the lorry and levelling will have to be done by hand. Your lorry driver will not like waiting while you do this; which brings me on to the main aspect of driver education.

Most lorry drops involve the driver taking a signature, opening the tailboard, tipping and driving away. If this is done with a boat then he will probably sink it and/or lose a significant part of your load overboard, so have no qualms about making him aware of this danger, and therefore his liability, should he not obey your instructions.

When the tailboard is opened, something like a tonne (almost the same as a ton!) will drop straight into your hold and so it is important that this goes centrally widthwise. Typically the lorry rear end needs to be overhanging your gunwale by about 1'6" to 2 feet (0.5 - 0.6m). Ensure that the tailboard is opened before the body is tipped. Be suspicious of any driver who won't do this or if nothing much comes out. It is a classic trick to take advantage of the inexperienced by "losing" a few hundredweight on a friend or "customer's" driveway. If you *are* suspicious incidentally contact the driver's employers immediately and be prepared to bag up the whole load immediately (with authenticated scales of course). This is a serious step and should not be taken lightly and I only mention it in case you wonder why your profit is not quite as great as expected!

As loading proceeds, the cargo will be coming from higher up in the lorry body and will therefore fly further and faster as it leaves the tailgate. This means you will have to move the boat out from the bank or the lorry further away from the edge. To help with this I have always had the offside sidecloth rigged to stop excess going over the edge and the inside sidecloth tied loosely to a couple of top planks laid on the bank away from the edge to catch anything trying to fall down the gap. Never tie these tight to anything on the bank as the boat will fall a couple or more feet with the loading. Tying to the top planks as described enables them to slide sideways but still keeps the cloths taut. Incidentally, cover your mast and stands with old sacks to protect your paintwork.

I mentioned earlier that your lorry driver will be used to a "drop and go" situation rather than careful boat loading. Emphasize that by cooperating with you he will be on his way faster and explain that the idea is for him to use his skill to get a steady stream of cargo into the boat's hold but that he will have to be ready to drop the wagon body immediately in an emergency should you signal it. Establish this signal before you start!

When loading is complete, the boat should be level across her beam and along her length or slightly down by the head. Make sure there is somewhere for'ard for a bilge pump incidentally. Not merely for tidiness, but also for your own convenience and safety, level the top of the mound(s) from gunwale to gunwale. This makes for easy walking about (and a place for Granny's deckchair or the kiddies toys!).

Loaded!

Assuming you can get away from the bank and into the channel (if not see "on becoming unstuck" in an earlier chapter) your vessel will have taken on a completely new "feel". This is what makes it all worthwhile and, if you've never steered a deeply loaded boat, you don't know what you're missing. It's like having your own personal floating island.

The first thing you will notice is that the whole thing seems a lot more stable. As you walk about, the boat won't rock so readily. It *will* rock just as much but will take so much longer doing it. In fact *everything* takes much longer, starting, turning and - most important of all - stopping. In an early chapter I described what I referred to as the boat's "longitudinal centre of gravity", this will now have moved. Going round bends will feel more like pushing a pea along with your nose. On the credit side, the boat will be much better at following the channel by herself but you will have much less room to move out of the way of others. Slow down, be polite to passing boaters and stories of channel hogging will not dog you or other innocent historic boaters.

Whilst effects of wind will be greatly reduced, effects of current will be enhanced but your greatly increased mass (and/or that of the boat!) will slow everything down. The counter current (ie the flow of water backwards along the hull from bow to stern) may seem greater but really it just occurs along a greater length. This is because your maximum draught will probably not be significantly increased, nor will your cross sectional area, but these factors will now apply along almost the whole length of your hull. The main significance of this is that objects underwater which you once bounced over with ease will now have to scrape all along your bottom. To say that your chances of getting cleanly through most bridgeholes are reduced is likely to be something of an understatement.

I have already covered most variations of steering and lock working. With a loaded boat everything just happens rather slower but with noticeably more force. Warnings I have given about trapped feet and fingers etc therefore apply with even greater importance. Strapping on gates and similar techniques require less speed. In fact more stopping time will have to be allowed generally. There are however a couple of distinct features about working through a lock with a loaded boat and with these I will conclude this guide.

When approaching a lock from downhill you may have noticed that, if the lock is empty, the bottom gates will open slightly as you approach. With a loaded boat this effect is greatly increased - so much so in fact that in some places such as the bottom lock at Stone or locks with bridges over the tails generally, you can actually open the gates without touching them. (This does no harm to the gates of course but be wary that the balance beams do not sweep the unwary off the lockside.) This even works when there is three or four inches difference in level but you need (a) confidence and (b) to be sure its *only* three or four inches difference...

Because of the water pushed ahead by the bows, this acts as an effective brake when entering from the downhill end and so you may find you can actually enter faster initially. From the uphill side, the restriction of the top cill will also slow you down more than usual **but** once over the cill, because of the deep water now beneath you, this braking effect suddenly ceases and reverse gear or a strap will still have to be employed to stop you hitting the bottom gates.

Chapter 12. IN CONCLUSION

I greatly enjoyed researching, and writing, the original articles and this book and, in so doing, I was able to clarify a lot of my own thinking on boatmanship. I was also forced to put into words a lot that had only existed as vague ideas in my head and hopefully this will now, in turn, improve my own techniques.

In many cases it is not practical to do things *exactly* as the working boaters. In others it is not *desirable* - they rarely had to contend with inexperienced other users - nor the Health and Safety measures in force today. Where possible I have shown how things now differ - usually for reasons of courtesy or lost lockside furniture - and so I hope that the old ways will not be completely lost but may survive by new adaptation.

It was said to me many years ago, by a very senior, and now sadly deceased old boatman, that "You never stop learning, y'know!". This was a source of pride to him, not of weakness as many might see it today. Well, I will readily admit that I am still learning as well, there are many out there who still know more than me, but I hope that through the medium of this book, I will have helped at least some of you, to learn some more too.

Chris N Deuchar, 1997

INDEX